52-Week Hockey Training

Don MacAdam
Gail Reynolds

Human Kinetics

Library of Congress Cataloging-in-Publication Data

MacAdam, Don, 1950-
    52-week hockey training / Don MacAdam, Gail Reynolds.
        p. cm
    ISBN 0-7360-4204-0
    1. Hockey--Training. 2. Physical education and training. I. Title: Fifty-two week
hockey training. II. Reynolds, Gail, 1949- III. Title.

GV848.3 .M32 2001
796.962--dc21

                                            2001039182

ISBN: 0-7360-4204-0

Developmental Editor: Leigh LaHood
Copyeditor: Bob Replinger
Proofreader: E.T. Cler
Graphic Designers: Fred Starbird and Nancy Rasmus
Graphic Artist: Francine Hamerski
Cover Designer: Jack W. Davis
Photographer (cover): Gary Cole
Photographer (interior): Gary Cole, unless otherwise noted
Art Managers: Craig Newsom and Carl Johnson
Illustrator: Tom Roberts
Printer: United Graphics

Human Kinetics books are available at special discounts for bulk purchase. Special editions or book excerpts can also be created to specification. For details, contact the Special Sales Manager at Human Kinetics.

Printed in the United States of America
10 9 8 7 6 5 4 3 2 1

Human Kinetics
Web site: www.humankinetics.com

United States: Human Kinetics
P.O. Box 5076
Champaign, IL 61825-5076
800-747-4457
e-mail: humank@hkusa.com

Canada: Human Kianetics
475 Devonshire Road Unit 100
Windsor, ON N8Y 2L5
800-465-7301 (in Canada only)
e-mail: orders@hkcanada.com

Europe: Human Kinetics
Units C2/C3 Wira Business Park
West Park Ring Road
Leeds LS16 6EB, United Kingdom
+44 (0) 113 278 1708
e-mail: hk@hkeurope.com

Australia: Human Kinetics
57A Price Avenue
Lower Mitcham, South Australia 5062
08 8277 1555
e-mail: liahka@senet.com.au

New Zealand: Human Kinetics
P.O. Box 105-231, Auckland Central
09-523-3462
e-mail: hkp@ihug.co.nz

Contents

Acknowledgments

A book is always the product of many contributing hands. Our thanks to Joanne Smith for her tireless assistance in preparing the manuscript for *52-Week Hockey Training*. Thanks also to Mark Simpson for wading through the action photo collection from his ever efficient PR office. And thank you, Mike Derecola, ATC, CSCS, for your generous donation of time to be the model for the exercise photo shoot and for your technical assistance. Leigh LaHood, you've been a pleasure to work with as an editor. And last but not least, our thanks to all the hockey players that contributed to the evolution of our training expertise.

Introduction

You can play ice hockey if you learn to perform the skills of the game, but you will play at your peak potential only if you get in shape to play the game.

What is your hockey goal? A solid NHL career? A college scholarship? The Olympics? You know what kind of skills it takes to compete at that level. You see the standard every time you watch an elite-level game. What you don't see is the work those players put in to ensure that they can use their skills whenever they want them. Pavel Bure isn't limited to one breakaway a game. He is in the kind of shape that allows him to capitalize on a breakaway opportunity whenever it presents itself. Absolutely, the man has superior skill, but he would be stoppable if he lacked the strength and stamina to ward off fatigue as the game progressed. You must train to be in condition to perform your skills at their peak, period in and period out, game in and game out, and through a grueling series of playoff games. *52-Week Hockey Training* is a day-by-day conditioning program that will get you in the kind of shape it takes to make the most of your hockey skills.

This book is for committed hockey players and their coaches. Whether male or female, amateur or professional, players who want to excel at the game must perform hockey skills quickly, powerfully, and repeatedly. What good is an accurate snap shot if you can't move quickly to get open to make the shot? What good is forcing overtime if you don't have the legs to continue to skate hard during the overtime? The power to move quickly and the stamina for sustained hard skating come not from practicing skills but from conditioning the muscles and cardiovascular system. *52-Week Hockey Training* will help you develop the strength, power, and endurance you need to produce peak performance.

Part I of the book presents daily conditioning workouts, including scheduled rest days, that will get and keep a player or team in excellent shape through a complete hockey year. Part II describes how to do each of the exercises and drills described in part I.

The *52-Week Hockey Training* program is divided into four seasons: off-season, preseason, in-season, and postseason. These divisions are necessary because training priorities change as the hockey year progresses. What gets you in shape is not the same as what keeps you in shape; what you need for playoffs is different from what you need to get started in training.

The hockey year begins with off-season training, which usually starts three to four months before any games begin. The training priority at this stage is to build a sound physical base. For instance, players ultimately want the elements of speed, power, and quickness to maximize their skill performance. But you can't train hard enough to maximize these attributes if you don't have good muscle strength, muscle endurance, flexibility, and aerobic endurance. You need to establish a base in those elements first just so you will be capable of doing quality speed, power, and quickness training.

Building a base is even more important if you are rehabilitating from an injury or if you need to overcome a weakness in past performance, like lead feet or a weak upper body. Off-season is the only time you have for quality catch-up.

After you establish your base, which usually takes 6 to 12 weeks depending on what kind of shape you were in to start with, you are ready for preseason training. The priority then becomes game readiness. This is a two-part challenge. First, you must build speed, power, and quickness. Second, you must ensure that your speed, power, and quickness are game specific and that they transfer to your skills. For instance, powerful forearms are wonderful, but they aren't much help to your game if you can't transfer their strength to an ability to release a quick snap shot on the fly.

In the off-season, off-ice training is appropriate, even preferable, for establishing the base elements. But to develop game readiness, you must train on-ice. The skills of hockey use your muscles, nerves, and joints in a way unlike any off-ice activity. You must train exactly what you need on-ice to have it when you want it. Close isn't good enough. In other words, if you train a quadriceps muscle to press your body weight over a three-second interval, you have only trained your quad muscle to fire at a measured pace. You have not trained it to perform repeatedly over fractions of a second to give you the explosive takeoff you want on-ice. Training at a deliberate pace develops better strength, but faster, more specific training is necessary to fine-tune muscles for on-ice skills. Game-specific training is critical to successful preseason training.

Once games begin, priorities change again for in-season training. Coaches want to focus on team tactics and strategies. The goal of conditioning becomes maintenance. During this period, game schedules typically interrupt ideal training schedules, especially when teams play more than two games a week. But if a team wants to play at its peak all season and be in top shape for a playoff schedule, players must train enough to maintain both the base and the game-specific elements of conditioning (speed, power, and quickness) throughout the season.

When games and playoffs are over, the postseason begins. Although players might wish that the postseason means they have a "do nothing" priority for a couple of months, the best rule to follow is the old adage that "a change is better than a rest." Even so, an initial short rest may be helpful. Postseason is the time to become healthy and refreshed.

For an overview of the four seasons of the hockey year, look at table I.1, the *52-Week* seasonal plan.

The time frames used in this seasonal plan are common to many teams. Of course, every hockey league runs on a different schedule. Some use 20-week game schedules; some use 30 weeks or more with playoffs. Some start games in August, others in October. The *52-Week Hockey Training* plan can be easily adapted, regardless of the length of your seasons.

Each week of the *52-Week* training plan is assigned a number. Week 18 is the most important because that is when scheduled games begin. To set the *52-Week* plan to suit your schedule, use the blank months column in table I.1 to write in the months that match your schedule. Begin with your in-season. For example,

Table I.1 *52-Week* Seasonal Plan

Season	Weeks	Months
Off-season	1, 2, 3, 4, 5, 6, 7, 8	
Preseason	9, 10, 11, 12, 13, 14, 15, 16, 17	
In-season	18, 19, 20, 21, 22	
	23, 24, 25, 26, 27	
	28, 29, 30, 31	
	32, 33, 34, 35	
	36, 37, 38, 39	
	40, 41, 42, 43, 44	
(Playoffs)	45, 46, 47, 48	
Postseason	49, 50, 51, 52	

if your game schedule starts in early October, you would place October opposite the block of weeks 18 to 22. Complete your in-season schedule, then work backward and forward from there. You will then have numbers for the weekly workouts that correspond to your schedule.

If the in-season of your league is shorter than the one in this seasonal plan, your postseason may start in week 47 rather than week 49. In that case, you could extend the postseason to 6 weeks, which is not excessive, and you would adjust the workouts accordingly. The key is to block off a minimum of 6 to 8 weeks for off-season base building and 8 to 10 weeks for preseason fine-tuning because it takes that long to attain a high level of conditioning.

Chapters 1 through 4 present specific conditioning workouts for each day of each week. The chapters and workouts run consecutively, starting with off-season training. All the exercises used in chapters 1 through 4 are explained or illustrated in part II, organized for easy reference into chapters for flexibility, muscle strength and endurance, aerobic endurance, speed, and power and quickness. Each of these chapters also presents alternative exercises for those used in the *52-Week* program. The alternatives can provide more variety in workouts, allow athletes to do extra work on weak areas, serve as substitute drills if ice is not available, or permit use of different equipment that may be available.

The *52-Week Hockey Training* program includes everything high-performance athletes need to get and stay in shape to play top-level amateur and professional hockey. The program uses basic exercise equipment but incorporates the most current and successful training techniques, such as plyometrics and fartlek. Because the program doesn't require special equipment, anyone who wants to get to an elite level can attain his or her goal. But if your team has access to a broader range of equipment than what this program requires, such as isokinetic machines, go ahead and substitute some of the exercises listed in part II or use exercises suggested by the equipment manufacturer. Just be sure to substitute one for one so that you receive all the necessary training.

The *52-Week* program starts with off-ice training and moves to on-ice sessions as the preseason evolves. This schedule reflects when most teams gain access to ice and when specificity of training becomes important in transferring what you have trained to hockey skills. If your team always has ice available, on-ice alternative exercises can be incorporated as soon as a fitness base is established. If your team doesn't have ice available as often as designated in the *52-Week* program, you can substitute off-ice alternative exercises from part II. This approach will compromise your training somewhat because it lacks specificity as the playing season draws near. You can partially compensate by doing as much speed and quickness training on-ice as possible once you gain access to ice in the late preseason. In addition, the *52-Week* plan provides combination fitness-skill drills to ensure transfer of fitness to skills. Using more combination exercises in practices than prescribed by the basic plan can also help compensate for limited access to ice.

The *52-Week* program is designed to make optimum use of practice and ice time for training. Ice time is at a premium for many teams. Coaches and players must spend time working on skill development, team strategies, and psychological preparation in addition to physical conditioning. The *52-Week* program provides high-level conditioning using on-ice sessions that are usually 10 to 20 minutes long, so they fit comfortably into normal practice time frames. Off-ice workouts are usually longer, at 60 to 90 minutes. If you have the time and inclination to do more conditioning than what the *52-Week* program recommends, you can selectively add alternative exercises as long as you do not exclude rest. If you overtrain, injury and slower progress usually result. Don't go overboard.

The *52-Week* program is designed for male and female hockey players of approximately age 15 and older. Individuals vary considerably in starting fitness level and in how quickly their bodies adapt and progress with training. For that reason, do not expect all team members to progress at precisely the pace of the program. The program presents ideal targets. A slightly overweight, previously injured player may wisely choose to lag behind the program targets for a time before eventually reaching the ideal levels. Use common sense in pushing progress. The effort must be a challenge for progression to occur, but creating undue fatigue hampers progress.

The question of whether all hockey players need the same training often comes up. All players, regardless of the position they play, need a high level of all aspects of fitness to play ice hockey well. This is partly because the game imposes a variety of physical demands on each player. More importantly, it is because elite hockey makes maximum use of speed, quickness, and power, regardless of position. You cannot fully train these aspects of performance without having a sound base in aerobics, muscle strength, muscle endurance, and flexibility. So whether you are a goaltender or a winger, a defenseman or a center, you must train all aspects of fitness. That said, in a game, forwards normally do more skating and shooting than defensemen, who usually do more hitting and quick maneuvering than goaltenders, who do little skating and plenty of quick moving. The style of the best forwards and defensemen is almost interchangeable. All have the ability to jump into the play, shoot, and check or back-check, as the case may be. So the training needs of all skaters are similar, leaving goaltenders as the only players who can make a case for less skating and more short, quick-burst training. Therefore, they are in need of more power and quickness and less speed training than the forwards and defensemen.

The *52-Week Hockey Training* program is designed to get all players into top shape, regardless of position, and then to provide specialized training for various positions. Initially, positional specialization is incorporated in the program as a matter of target level. To that end, goaltenders must push themselves to the maximum quickness targets, wingers must push to the highest speed targets, defensemen must push to maximize upper-body strength and foot quickness, and scorers must maximize hand quickness. As specificity becomes important in the preseason, position-specific drills are included in the training program, particularly for goaltenders. These drills are also used periodically in-season to maintain speed, power, and quickness in position-specific skills.

Besides preparing yourself for the requirements of your position, you may choose to do supplementary fitness training for several reasons. You may simply be highly motivated to improve, or you may be trying to return from an injury. Perhaps you realize that you've become an average player and decide that's not good enough. Whatever the reason, you can select drills or exercises from the alternative listings in part II for extra work in areas you want to develop to a higher level. For instance, suppose you're recovering from a shoulder injury. By using a wider variety of muscle strength, muscle endurance, and flexibility exercises for the shoulder, you can secure a quicker and more thorough recovery. Perhaps you are overweight from an overly long and indulgent postseason. Additional aerobic, muscle endurance, or aerobic-speed combination exercises will hasten your weight loss. Perhaps you are a defenseman who needs to add functional weight. Additional strength training will help you add the right kind of weight. Or maybe you're like the wise but aging (translate "slowing") Detroit Red Wings defenseman who learned from the authors some quick-feet drills that helped him extend a career of 900-plus games to more than 1,000. There are many good reasons to supplement your training. Part II provides numerous options.

An exercise and drill directory on pages xii-xv provides a convenient reference for finding out how to do any exercise in the book. All exercises and drills in the *52-Week* plan, as well as the alternative exercises, are explained.

Along with all this training, a sound nutritional program is crucial, although that aspect of your preparation is beyond the scope of this book. If you are unsure about what you should be eating and drinking, consult a sports nutrition specialist. You don't need drugs to maximize hockey performance, but to train hard you need quality food and water.

Also beyond the scope of this book but crucial to the success of your training and your hockey is goal setting. Set reasonable targets throughout your program and evaluate your progress. Monthly goals and checks will help you stay on track.

Finally, to begin any training session, be sure to warm up properly. That means doing 5 to 15 minutes of loose, easy, flowing activity that uses all the major muscle groups. For example, you might walk using exaggerated arm swings and then jog. You could also use a low-resistance setting on a rowing machine. Or you could skate with exaggerated arm swings, skating forward, skating backward, and doing some light lateral work. If you follow this by doing loose head, shoulder, trunk, and leg circles and stretches to ensure that no joints are tight, you should be loose and warm enough for a good workout.

So warm up and let your best hockey season ever begin.

Exercise and Drill Finder

Exercise or drill	Training element	Page number
Arm step-ups	Power and quickness	172
Back extension, stable	Muscle strength	119
Back extension, unstable	Muscle strength	128
Back flys	Muscle endurance	152
Behind-the-neck military press	Muscle strength	138
Bench press	Muscle strength	115
Bent-over rowing	Muscle strength	139
Biceps curls, stable	Muscle strength	117
Biceps curls, unstable	Muscle strength	124
Box skate	Power and quickness	182
Bridging	Muscle strength	126
Bridging with rotation	Muscle strength	126
Burpees	Muscle endurance	150
Calisthenics	Muscle strength	132
Calf stretches	Flexibility	110
Center shuttle	Power and quickness	173
Chin-ups	Muscle strength	124
Circle shuttle	Power and quickness	173
Close-grip bench	Muscle strength	141
Continuous scrimmage	Speed/skill	166
3-on-3 cross-zone drill	Speed/skill	165
Curl bar	Muscle strength	143
Deadlift	Muscle strength	135
Defense get-out drill	Speed	163
Defense net drill	Speed	163
Defense walk-and-shoot drill	Power and quickness	175
Dips (bar)	Muscle strength	144
Dips (bench)	Muscle endurance	149
Double step-ups	Power and quickness	181

Key to Diagrams

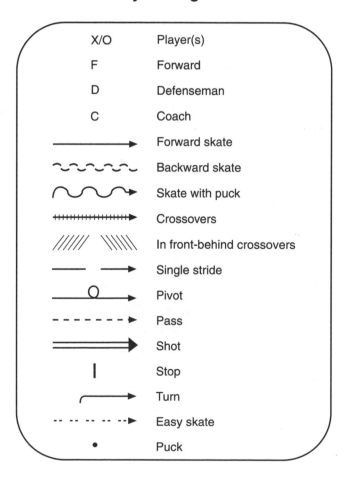

X/O	Player(s)
F	Forward
D	Defenseman
C	Coach
⟶	Forward skate
∿∿∿∿	Backward skate
∿⟶	Skate with puck
++++⟶	Crossovers
///// \\\\\	In front-behind crossovers
— ⟶	Single stride
—Q⟶	Pivot
- - - - ▸	Pass
⟹	Shot
I	Stop
⌐⟶	Turn
-- - -- - ->▸	Easy skate
•	Puck

Year-Round Hockey Training Plan

Part I presents a full year of daily hockey training workouts that will help any serious hockey player maximize his or her on-ice performance. Workouts begin in chapter 1 with the off-season when players build the physical base they need as a foundation for more specific hockey training. Then speed, power, and quickness training starts in chapter 2, the preseason. These are the fitness elements that lead to high-performance hockey. Once the game schedule begins in chapter 3, training for all fitness elements is adjusted so players can maintain the high level of fitness they established during the previous two training seasons. Fitness is maintained throughout the in-season so that by playoffs, game performance can peak. Finally, players reach the postseason in chapter 4. Training sessions then focus on rest and recovery.

Workouts throughout the four seasons can be adjusted to suit varying lengths of seasons. The program includes position-specific and skill-specific training sessions, so players can use their fitness to improve their unique skills and game performance.

Chapter

1

Off-Season Workouts

"You are what you are when no one is looking."—**Author unknown**

Off-season is the time of the hockey year when many hockey players are on their own. Your coach may have provided a training program for you to follow, but no one will be pushing you daily or looking over your shoulder. Your coach just expects you to train and stay in shape.

If you want to be a high-performance hockey player, you must train through the off-season. The off-season is the only season in which you have enough time to build a fitness base. Just as a house needs a foundation, you need a fitness foundation. Ultimately, you want speed, power, and quickness for high-performance hockey. You only get that combination by building on a foundation of aerobics, muscle strength, muscle endurance, and flexibility. For instance, to improve speed and quickness, you must repeatedly push the limits of the speed and quickness that you already have. You can't do that unless you can recover sufficiently between repeats. Aerobic endurance gives you a recovery system. To improve power, you need a combination of strength and elasticity in muscles and joints, which come from muscle strength and flexibility training. Few actions in hockey are executed only once; most are repeated many times at high tempo, like the skating stride. These actions require muscle endurance. Therefore, a hockey player needs a fitness foundation in aerobics, muscle strength, muscle endurance, and flexibility. The off-season is the time to build that foundation.

To establish a good base, a hockey player must normally train each of these elements for 6 to 8 weeks, three to five times per week. But if you start with an unusually low aerobic capacity or if an injury has left muscles weak and joints with a poor range of motion, you may need as much as 12 weeks of base training. The off-season is your single best chance to eliminate the weakness of a former injury, like a chronic groin problem, or to neutralize a weakness in your performance, like slow acceleration. In the off-season you have the time to do the necessary catch-up.

Once you establish a good base in the four fitness elements, you gain more than just the ability to train harder to improve your speed, power, and quickness. Having a strong aerobic, muscle, and flexibility base reduces the risk of many types of injuries from both training and playing. Fatigue-related injuries, sprains, and strains are less likely to occur. If you do become injured, a strong aerobic, strength, and flexibility base usually facilitates recovery from injuries so that you can return to the game more quickly. One well-known example of this is Steve Yzerman of the Detroit Red Wings. Although he has suffered serious accidental injuries, he has come back seemingly stronger every time. Yzerman has always been known to take his training seriously.

Consider each of the base elements of training individually.

Aerobics

Aerobic endurance is the ability of your heart, lungs, and blood system to feed your muscles efficiently and flush out the garbage that results from exercise. If you have aerobic endurance, you can perform at a high level all game long because fatigue from a diminishing fuel supply and accumulating garbage doesn't set in. Aerobic endurance also enables you to recover more completely when you take breaks, such as when you coast around between whistles or when you sit after a shift or between periods. Besides helping you perform and recover more efficiently during games, cardiovascular efficiency and recovery enable you to train hard to develop the speed, power, and quickness you need for playing high-intensity, quality games. You can't repeat high-intensity efforts if you can't recover in the pauses between those efforts. Like most players, you have probably had to do "suicide" sprints at some time and have felt your performance in successive all-out efforts deteriorate as your legs began to feel like dead weights. That decline in performance is the result of low fuel levels and accumulating garbage in your system. An efficient aerobic system refuels and flushes your muscles during the rest after each suicide sprint. It does the same thing on whistle stops during shifts, between shifts, and between periods and games. The ability to recover

© Frank DiBrango

A strong base of aerobic fitness enables you to skate and play hard during the whole game.

quickly, which results from having a good aerobic base, is essential to quality training and high-level game performance for hockey players.

You improve your aerobic system by challenging it to withstand brisk, long-lasting, whole-body, continuous, rhythmic activity. Running, cycling, rowing, in-line skating, and cross-country skiing all meet aerobic training requirements. The aerobic training program used in *52-Week Hockey Training* allows you to use any of these activities. Water running is also listed as an aerobic activity in the *52-Week* program. Although hockey players are more familiar with frozen water than flowing water, water running provides an excellent workout for the muscles of the upper and lower body as well as the cardiovascular system. Water running is particularly valuable when a player's joints could benefit from reduced impact, such as following an injury or late in the season when wear and tear begin to take a toll. In choosing an activity for aerobic training, consider the weather, your preferences, and what equipment you have available. Preferably, you would use a variety of the suggested aerobic activities.

The *52-Week* off-season aerobic program is a progressive, nine-level program that will safely and effectively take you to an aerobic level that provides a sound base for training speed, power, and quickness. It will give you a high-performance aerobic capacity that resists fatigue and provides excellent recovery. See table 1.1 for the progressive aerobic training program.

Table 1.1 Progressive Aerobic Training Program

Level	Activity: running, cycling, rowing, in-line skating, cross-country skiing, water running
1	20 min easy
2	20 min easy, 5 min strong
3	20 min easy, 10 min strong
4	15 min easy, 15 min strong
5	15 min easy, 20 min strong
6	15 min easy, 25 min strong
7	10 min easy, 30 min strong
8	5 min easy, 35 min strong
9	5 min easy, 40 min strong

You will notice that pace is specified at every level of the progressive aerobic training program—some as "easy," some as "strong." Successful aerobic development requires you to understand how to use pace effectively when training. Chapter 7 defines easy and strong paces and provides a scale that will help you identify the appropriate pace. Chapter 7 also explains how to adapt and progress through the nine-level program if the targets used in the daily workouts are not appropriate for you. Injury and initial fitness level are two factors that commonly require adjustment in progression.

Muscle Strength and Endurance

The more strength you have available to perform hockey skills, the more likely you are to perform those skills at a high level. For instance, a weak set of leg muscles results in poor starts and stops in hockey. Similarly, the more able you are to perform skills at a high level repeatedly over the course of practices and games, the more likely it is that you will dominate your opponents. Picture Scott Stevens clearing the front of the net. He is strong enough to do it well and has enough muscle endurance to do it repeatedly.

Muscle strength and endurance benefit not only skating and defending skills but also shooting and passing skills. Think back to how you played hockey when you were 11 years old. How soft were your shots and passes? How did that affect your accuracy and the speed with which you could shoot? As your strength improved, so did your control of the puck and your ability to exert control quickly. Muscle strength and muscle endurance are part of the foundation for building solid hockey skills.

The *52-Week* muscle strength program is based on a core list of exercises that work all the muscles and muscle groups you need to perform hockey skills successfully. The program includes upper-body work for establishing a good base for shooting and defending skills, lower-body work for use in skating and maneuvering skills, and torso exercises that provide the stability required for

Your shooting and passing skills benefit from muscle strength training because you gain greater control of the puck.

executing most hockey skills. The program also balances the muscle groups so that players will not become predisposed to injury. Injury commonly occurs when one side of a joint is made strong but the other side remains weak. Players often neglect to develop the muscle on one side of a joint because they feel they don't need it to execute a specific skill. For example, you know you need quadriceps muscle strength for strong skating strides. To provide stability to your hip and knee, however, you must also strengthen the hamstrings and inner and outer thigh muscles. A strong quad and weak muscles surrounding these joints is an invitation to injury. See table 1.2 for the exercises that constitute your off-season strength-training program.

The *52-Week* program begins with a strength focus and evolves to a power focus because power is how players most often use strength in hockey. A defenseman has to shove a forward out of the slot quickly (with power), not at the pace of a steady bench press. The program begins with slower lifts and presses because that approach is an effective way to improve strength. The tempo then picks up to develop power using that new strength.

Table 1.2 Core Strength-Training Program and Unstable Workout

Core strength program	Unstable workout
Upper body	**Upper body on ball**
Bench press	Dumbbell press
Incline bench press	Dumbbell pullover
Military press	Chin-ups
Pull-downs	Biceps curls
Biceps curls	Triceps curls
Triceps curls	Wrist curls
Wrist curls	
Torso	**Torso on ball**
Sit-ups	Bridging
Back extension	Bridging with rotation
Lateral raises	Supine with feet on ball
	Back extension
Lower body	**Lower body on ball**
Squats	One-leg squat
Leg flexion	One-leg curl
Leg extension	Hip flexion
Heel raises	Hip extension
Lateral leg pulls (inside and outside)	Wall squats

The *52-Week* strength program uses free weights for training because they are often all that is available to hockey teams. If your training center provides other types of strength-training equipment, you can substitute exercises that work the same muscle group. Just be sure not to omit any muscle groups. Chapter 6 provides some suggestions for alternate exercises for a variety of muscle groups.

You'll notice that table 1.2 includes a list of exercises for unstable workouts, which start in week 7 of the off-season. This advanced form of strength training is useful for hockey because the player must make greater use of stabilizing muscles during an exercise, similar to the way the player would use the muscles to execute hockey skills like stopping and turning. Unstable workouts require a good strength base and a special piece of equipment, the Swiss ball. If you are not ready to advance to this type of workout or if you do not have the equipment, use the core strength program throughout the season. Make it a goal to add unstable workouts next season.

Resistance and tempo are key factors in strength improvement. These factors vary throughout the off-season workouts to provide safe progress toward a high level of strength specifically designed to improve hockey skills. If you are not familiar with how to establish an appropriate resistance and how to use the tempo designations for effective training, be sure to check chapter 6 before starting your strength training.

You must develop muscle endurance along with muscle strength so that you can use your strength repeatedly. Your leg muscles need endurance to stride repeatedly throughout a shift. A defenseman needs endurance in the upper-body muscles to keep a persistent forward away from the front of the net.

The *52-Week* off-season muscle endurance program consists of a core group of exercises that involve the muscles frequently used for endurance in hockey. The stabilizing muscles of the torso are often called upon to perform the repetitive actions of hockey. The torso stabilizes the body during stops, starts, skating, passing, shooting, fending off, and even sitting on the bench. Therefore, the torso muscles are the focus of the *52-Week* muscle endurance program. The arm muscles perform less repetition in hockey and instead use power more frequently. The leg muscles receive sufficient repetitive challenge through aerobic training, unless you canoe for aerobic training. See table 1.3 for the muscle endurance training program.

Table 1.3   Core Muscle Endurance Training Program

Twist sit-ups

Knee tucks

Trunk lifts

Leg lifts

Push-ups

Dips

Lateral curls

Burpees

Slider board (optional)

Repetitions help muscles improve endurance, so the training program specifies a variety of repetitions, depending on the workout. Tempo is also important because it eliminates momentum, which can minimize the training effect. The workouts specify tempos for the different repetitions. See chapter 6 for tips on how to perform the repetitions at the designated tempos so that you obtain the best results from your training.

The *52-Week* muscle endurance program requires minimal equipment so that equipment availability (or lack of it) is not a limitation to training. As with strength training, the player can use alternative exercises using the same muscle groups for variety or if specific equipment is available. See chapter 6 for suggestions on exercise substitutions.

Flexibility

Flexibility is what provides fluid motion and minimal risk of injury. Picture the fluid skating strides of Wayne Gretzky, Mike Modano, or Joe Sakic. Flexibility also provides range of motion and elasticity, which are crucial factors in power generation. The power of a Brett Hull slap shot comes not from strength alone. Flexibility is of considerable value to hockey players.

Hockey players need a good range of motion in every major muscle group and elasticity around every joint in the body because hockey skills use virtually every muscle of the body. You want shoulder and torso muscles to stretch for sufficient back swing and to recoil to generate a powerful slap shot. When you assume an unusual leg position in a hit or fall, you want groin muscles to extend easily and return to normal position without tearing. You want forearm muscles to let your wrists snap through a decent range of motion to execute a powerful snap shot or a quick, accurate pass. Hockey requires players to have good overall flexibility. The *52-Week* flexibility program gives you a wide range of motion and elasticity for the total body by using packages of sequence stretches. See table 1.4 for the stretch sequences of the *52-Week* flexibility program.

© Rob Tringali Jr./SportsChrome USA

Flexibility training allows for more fluid motion in your skating strides, like those of the Avalanche's Joe Sakic.

Table 1.4 Flexibility Program

Squat sequence
Squat
Forward bend
Uncurl

Lateral and shoulder sequence
Lateral lunge, extend
Uncurl
Side bends
Torso twist
Shoulder presses

Seven-point sequence
Calf stretch
Knee lunge
Hip stretch
Groin stretch
Quad stretch
Abdominal stretch
Back relaxer

Wrist and ankle sequence
Flex
Extend
Pronate
Supinate
Circles

Stretch sequences are used throughout the *52-Week* program because they allow you to work more segments of muscles than static stretching exercises do. For example, a typical static calf stretch stretches just the upper segment of the calf muscle. A sequence calf stretch moves the stretch from top to bottom of the calf. In addition, sequence stretching is more likely to include all muscle groups, producing a whole-body workout.

Alternative exercises can be substituted for segments in the sequences. Chapter 5 contains substitute suggestions that will alter the flow of the sequence but be just as effective. Be sure that the substitute exercise stretches the same muscle group as the original exercise. See chapter 5 for precisely how to do each sequence if you have not done sequence stretching before.

The *52-Week* program advises athletes to use the stretch-relaxation technique throughout flexibility training. Other stretching techniques can improve flexibility, but the stretch-relaxation technique provides quicker improvements in range of motion and more effective reduction of muscle soreness following heavy workouts. See chapter 5 for how to do stretch-relaxation if you are unfamiliar with the technique.

The preceding programs for aerobics, muscle strength, muscle endurance, and flexibility provide what you need to begin your off-season workouts. Post each of the programs on the wall where you work out. Then put the daily workout details, like number of repetitions, resistance, and tempo, on the chalkboard. Remember that the daily program sets ideal paces and targets. For optimum improvement you may have to modify the paces and targets to progress at a rate appropriate for you.

The following *52-Week* off-season workouts take you through the first eight weeks of your year-round training program. As you go through these programs, see the appropriate chapter in part II for an explanation of terms that may be unfamiliar.

Off-Season Workouts

Purpose
- Build a fitness base
- Eliminate fundamental weaknesses

Focus
- Aerobic endurance
- Muscle strength and endurance
- Flexibility

Reminders
- 4-2-4 tempo = 4-second initial move–2-second hold–4-second return to start position
- HRR = hold–relax–repeat
- 1/6 sec = one complete cycle of the exercise takes 6 seconds

Week 1 Off-Season

	Program/activity	Sets/repetitions
MONDAY	**STRENGTH**	
	Core program	3 sets, 8-10 reps, 4-2-4 tempo
	FLEXIBILITY	
	Sequence program	2 × 30 sec HRR

	Program/activity	Sets/repetitions
TUESDAY	**AEROBIC**	
	Level 1	
	MUSCLE ENDURANCE	
	Core program	3 sets of 20 at 1/6 sec
	FLEXIBILITY	
	Sequence program	2 × 30 sec HRR

	Program/activity	Sets/repetitions
WED	**STRENGTH**	
	Core program	3 sets, 8-10 reps, 4-2-4 tempo
	FLEXIBILITY	
	Sequence program	2 × 30 sec HRR

	Program/activity	Sets/repetitions
THURSDAY	**AEROBIC**	
	Level 2	
	MUSCLE ENDURANCE	
	Core program	2 sets of 30 at 1/4 sec
	FLEXIBILITY	
	Sequence program	2 × 30 sec HRR

	Program/activity	Sets/repetitions
FRIDAY	**STRENGTH**	
	Core program	3 sets, 8-10 reps, 4-2-4 tempo
	FLEXIBILITY	
	Sequence program	2 × 30 sec HRR

SATURDAY	**AEROBIC**	
	Level 3	
	MUSCLE ENDURANCE	
	Core program	To exhaustion at 1/sec
	FLEXIBILITY	
	Sequence program	2 × 30 sec HRR

SUN	**DAY OFF**

Week 2 Off-Season

	Program/activity	Sets/repetitions
MONDAY	**STRENGTH**	
	Core program	3 sets, 8-10 reps, 4-2-4 tempo
	FLEXIBILITY	
	Sequence program	2 × 30 sec HRR

TUESDAY	**AEROBIC**	
	Level 3	
	MUSCLE ENDURANCE	
	Core program	3 sets of 20 at 1/6 sec
	FLEXIBILITY	
	Sequence program	2 × 30 sec HRR

WED	**STRENGTH**	
	Core program	3 sets, 8-10 reps, 4-2-4 tempo
	FLEXIBILITY	
	Sequence program	2 × 30 sec HRR

Program/activity	Sets/repetitions
THURSDAY	
AEROBIC	
Level 4	
MUSCLE ENDURANCE	
Core program	2 sets of 30 at 1/4 sec
FLEXIBILITY	
Sequence program	2 × 30 sec HRR

FRIDAY	
STRENGTH	
Core program	3 sets, 8-10 reps, 4-2-4 tempo
FLEXIBILITY	
Sequence program	2 × 30 sec HRR

SATURDAY	
AEROBIC	
Level 4	
MUSCLE ENDURANCE	
Core program	To exhaustion at 1/sec
FLEXIBILITY	
Sequence program	2 × 30 sec HRR

SUN	**DAY OFF**

Week 3 Off-Season

	Program/activity	Sets/repetitions
MONDAY	**STRENGTH**	
	Core program	3 sets, 8-10 reps, 4-2-4 tempo
	FLEXIBILITY	
	Sequence program	2 × 30 sec HRR

	Program/activity	Sets/repetitions
TUESDAY	**AEROBIC**	
	Level 5	
	MUSCLE ENDURANCE	
	Core program	3 sets of 20 at 1/6 sec
	FLEXIBILITY	
	Sequence program	2 × 30 sec HRR

	Program/activity	Sets/repetitions
WED	**STRENGTH**	
	Core program	3 sets, 8-10 reps, 4-2-4 tempo
	FLEXIBILITY	
	Sequence program	2 × 30 sec HRR

	Program/activity	Sets/repetitions
THURSDAY	**AEROBIC**	
	Level 4	
	MUSCLE ENDURANCE	
	Core program	2 sets of 30 at 1/4 sec
	FLEXIBILITY	
	Sequence program	2 × 30 sec HRR

	Program/activity	Sets/repetitions
FRIDAY	**STRENGTH**	
	Core program	3 sets, 8-10 reps, 4-2-4 tempo
	FLEXIBILITY	
	Sequence program	2 × 30 sec HRR

SATURDAY	Program/activity	Sets/repetitions
	AEROBIC	
	Level 5	
	MUSCLE ENDURANCE	
	Core program	To exhaustion at 1/sec
	FLEXIBILITY	
	Sequence program	2 × 30 sec HRR

SUN	
	DAY OFF

Week 4 Off-Season

MONDAY	Program/activity	Sets/repetitions
	STRENGTH	
	Core program	3 sets, 8-10 reps, 4-2-4 tempo
	FLEXIBILITY	
	Sequence program	2 × 30 sec HRR

TUESDAY		
	AEROBIC	
	Level 6	
	MUSCLE ENDURANCE	
	Core program	3 sets of 20 at 1/6 sec
	FLEXIBILITY	
	Sequence program	2 × 30 sec HRR

WED		
	STRENGTH	
	Core program	3 sets, 8-10 reps, 4-2-4 tempo
	FLEXIBILITY	
	Sequence program	2 × 30 sec HRR

THURSDAY	AEROBIC	
	Level 5	
	MUSCLE ENDURANCE	
	Core program	2 sets of 30 at 1/4 sec
	FLEXIBILITY	
	Sequence program	2 × 30 sec HRR

FRIDAY	STRENGTH	
	Core program	3 sets, 8-10 reps, 4-2-4 tempo
	FLEXIBILITY	
	Sequence program	2 × 30 sec HRR

SATURDAY	AEROBIC	
	Level 6	
	MUSCLE ENDURANCE	
	Core program	To exhaustion at 1/sec
	FLEXIBILITY	
	Sequence program	2 × 30 sec HRR

SUN	DAY OFF

Week 5 Off-Season

	Program/activity	Sets/repetitions
MONDAY	**STRENGTH**	
	Core program	3 sets, 8-10 reps, 4-2-4 tempo
	FLEXIBILITY	
	Sequence program	2 × 30 sec HRR

	Program/activity	Sets/repetitions
TUESDAY	**AEROBIC**	
	Level 7	
	MUSCLE ENDURANCE	
	Core program	3 sets of 20 at 1/6 sec
	FLEXIBILITY	
	Sequence program	2 × 30 sec HRR

	Program/activity	Sets/repetitions
WED	**STRENGTH**	
	Core program	3 sets, 8-10 reps, 4-2-4 tempo
	FLEXIBILITY	
	Sequence program	2 × 30 sec HRR

	Program/activity	Sets/repetitions
THURSDAY	**AEROBIC**	
	Level 6	
	MUSCLE ENDURANCE	
	Core program	2 sets of 30 at 1/4 sec
	FLEXIBILITY	
	Sequence program	2 × 30 sec HRR

	Program/activity	Sets/repetitions
FRIDAY	**STRENGTH**	
	Core program	3 sets, 8-10 reps, 4-2-4 tempo
	FLEXIBILITY	
	Sequence program	2 × 30 sec HRR

	Program/activity	Sets/repetitions
SATURDAY	**AEROBIC**	
	Level 7	
	MUSCLE ENDURANCE	
	Core program	To exhaustion at 1/sec
	FLEXIBILITY	
	Sequence program	2 × 30 sec HRR

SUN	DAY OFF

Week 6 Off-Season

	Program/activity	Sets/repetitions
MONDAY	**STRENGTH**	
	Core program	3 sets, 6-8 reps, 6-3-1 tempo
	FLEXIBILITY	
	Sequence program	2 × 30 sec HRR

	Program/activity	Sets/repetitions
TUESDAY	**AEROBIC**	
	Level 8	
	MUSCLE ENDURANCE	
	Core program	3 sets of 20 at 1/6 sec
	FLEXIBILITY	
	Sequence program	2 × 30 sec HRR

	Program/activity	Sets/repetitions
WED	**STRENGTH**	
	Core program	3 sets, 6-8 reps, 6-3-1 tempo
	FLEXIBILITY	
	Sequence program	2 × 30 sec HRR

	Program/activity	Sets/repetitions
THURSDAY	**AEROBIC**	
	Level 7	
	MUSCLE ENDURANCE	
	Core program	2 sets of 30 at 1/4 sec
	FLEXIBILITY	
	Sequence program	2 × 30 sec HRR

FRIDAY	**STRENGTH**	
	Core program	3 sets, 6-8 reps, 6-3-1 tempo
	FLEXIBILITY	
	Sequence program	2 × 30 sec HRR

SATURDAY	**AEROBIC**	
	Level 8	
	MUSCLE ENDURANCE	
	Core program	To exhaustion at 1/sec
	FLEXIBILITY	
	Sequence program	2 × 30 sec HRR

SUN	**DAY OFF**

Week 7 Off-Season

	Program/activity	Sets/repetitions
MONDAY	**STRENGTH**	
	Core program	3 sets, 6-8 reps, 6-3-1 tempo
	FLEXIBILITY	
	Sequence program	2 × 30 sec HRR

	Program/activity	Sets/repetitions
TUESDAY	**AEROBIC**	
	Level 9	
	MUSCLE ENDURANCE	
	Core program	3 sets of 20 at 1/6 sec
	FLEXIBILITY	
	Sequence program	2 × 30 sec HRR

	Program/activity	Sets/repetitions
WED	**STRENGTH**	
	Unstable workout	3 sets, 6-8 reps, 6-3-1 tempo
	FLEXIBILITY	
	Sequence program	2 × 30 sec HRR

	Program/activity	Sets/repetitions
THURSDAY	**AEROBIC**	
	Level 8	
	MUSCLE ENDURANCE	
	Core program	2 sets of 30 at 1/4 sec
	FLEXIBILITY	
	Sequence program	2 × 30 sec HRR

	Program/activity	Sets/repetitions
FRIDAY	**STRENGTH**	
	Core program	3 sets, 6-8 reps, 6-3-1 tempo
	FLEXIBILITY	
	Sequence program	2 × 30 sec HRR

Program/activity	Sets/repetitions
SATURDAY	
AEROBIC	
Level 9	
MUSCLE ENDURANCE	
Core program	To exhaustion at 1/sec
FLEXIBILITY	
Sequence program	2 × 30 sec HRR

SUN	DAY OFF

Week 8 Off-Season

Program/activity	Sets/repetitions
MONDAY	
STRENGTH	
Core program	3 sets, 6-8 reps, 6-3-1 tempo
FLEXIBILITY	
Sequence program	2 × 30 sec HRR

Program/activity	Sets/repetitions
TUESDAY	
AEROBIC	
Level 9	
MUSCLE ENDURANCE	
Core program	3 sets of 20 at 1/6 sec
FLEXIBILITY	
Sequence program	2 × 30 sec HRR

Program/activity	Sets/repetitions
WED	
STRENGTH	
Unstable workout	3 sets, 6-8 reps, 6-3-1 tempo
FLEXIBILITY	
Sequence program	2 × 30 sec HRR

THURSDAY	AEROBIC	
	Level 9	
	MUSCLE ENDURANCE	
	Core program	2 sets of 30 at 1/4 sec
	FLEXIBILITY	
	Sequence program	2 × 30 sec HRR

FRIDAY	STRENGTH	
	Core program	3 sets, 6-8 reps, 6-3-1 tempo
	FLEXIBILITY	
	Sequence program	2 × 30 sec HRR

SATURDAY	AEROBIC	
	Level 9	
	MUSCLE ENDURANCE	
	Core program	To exhaustion at 1/sec
	FLEXIBILITY	
	Sequence program	2 × 30 sec HRR

SUN	DAY OFF

Chapter 2

Preseason Workouts

"The will to win is not nearly so important as the will to prepare to win."—**Bear Bryant**

The preseason is your opportunity to determine how well you will prepare to win in the coming season. If you established a good foundation in the off-season, you are ready to train speed, power, and quickness, the essential elements to winning hockey. In the preseason you begin to focus on training muscles and movements specific to hockey, rather than working on the base-building elements that were your off-season focus. You need considerable will and determination to train speed, power, quickness, and specificity. The training is hard, but it will optimize the use of your skills better than any other aspect of hockey training.

"Then why didn't we start with this stuff?" you may ask. The answer is that you weren't ready. Your muscles and cardiovascular system (heart, lungs, and blood) didn't have the fuel-supply system, the recovery system, or the muscle machinery and range to do speed, power, quickness, and specificity training effectively. If you completed the *52-Week* off-season program, you will have the structure and efficiency to do the high-intensity training required to improve speed, power, and quickness.

You have to maintain your aerobic, muscle strength, muscle endurance, and flexibility base during the preseason or you'll lose the high level of fitness you attained. Both your training for speed, power, and quickness and your game performance will suffer as a result of letting things slip. Luckily, maintenance of the base fitness elements takes considerably less time and effort than building them. One or two sessions a week, with three on occasion, are sufficient. Note that it is still best to do flexibility training daily at the end of every practice or workout. Daily stretching tends to reduce the soreness that is common with speed and power training, and it relaxes muscles and maintains elasticity around joints after the muscles have been tightened by the daily workout, practice, or game.

© Don Smith/SportsChrome USA

Work on speed and quickness training in the preseason so that you can accelerate and hold your speed like Paul Kariya.

Speed and quickness training must occur before the game schedule begins. Speed takes a long time to improve, and each speed session requires a 48-hour recovery period, which is not often available in most game schedules. Just maintaining what you have developed is difficult enough during the playing season.

Quickness, on the other hand, improves rapidly, and you can train it daily. The difficulty comes in adapting your skills to the higher speeds. You don't want your shot and pass accuracy to go in a funk in the middle of a playoff run because you improved your quickness. Consequently, you should master the high-speed skills by the time games start. You accomplish that by doing all your heavy speed and quickness training in the preseason.

So dig out your will to prepare to win. Do the training it takes to get your foot speed and acceleration up to that of Paul Kariya. Do the training it takes to generate power in your shots to match that of Al MacInnis and Brett Hull. Do the training it takes to have the goaltending agility of Dominik Hasek or Curtis Joseph.

Look at the specific speed, power, and quickness information below. Then start your preseason program. The specificity you need is built into the training program for each element as the preseason workouts go from off-ice to on-ice.

Speed

Speed allows forwards to play end-to-end hockey at the same high pace throughout a shift. Speed lets you outrace an opponent for position, loose pucks, and overtime wins. Speed training lets you play high-intensity hockey every shift, all game long.

Speed is different from power or quickness. Speed is sustained high intensity. A defenseman must have speed to be part of a rush down ice and then immediately rush back because the play was broken up and the opposition is getting a breakaway. That defenseman can't afford to go at moderate intensity part of the way. Technically, speed comes from muscles burning high-octane sugar-based fuel that is stored inside the muscles. But this process produces a negative exhaust called lactic acid. Once that fuel runs low and the acid level becomes high, speed wanes. Your legs feel like lead, and your lungs burn trying to get some goods to the muscles and get the garbage out. Power and quickness, on the other hand, occur at higher intensity. The muscle uses a more explosive fuel but it only lasts a short time. For example, an aggressive stop and start requires power. To follow that with hard skating, you have to settle in to a slightly lesser intensity, which is speed. Your muscles switch from using explosive fuel for power to high-octane fuel for speed.

The only players who do not need considerable speed work are goaltenders. Most of their high-intensity efforts during the game last less than 10 seconds, a power time frame within the supply of explosive fuel. Power and quickness training, therefore, is a higher priority for goaltenders than is speed training. Goaltenders must perform some speed work, however, so that they can handle the sustained scrambles that occasionally occur around the net. Therefore, the *52-Week* preseason program begins with all players working to establish a functional speed base. For goalies, speed workouts are then reduced, and power and quickness workouts dominate.

Speed training begins off-ice using running, hills, stairs, or a stationary bike. These methods permit easier manipulation of intensity, which is what makes speed improve. Initially, you are likely to coast if you use only skating drills to train speed. Once you become familiar with the pace that is required, on-ice speed training becomes effective.

The final requirement of speed training is learning to execute skills at those high speeds. This type of training won't improve your speed; it will simply improve your ability to execute skills at high speeds. Anyone can learn to pass the puck accurately at a deliberate pace. But if you lose accuracy when you pick up the pace, your speed has no value. The *52-Week* program is designed to build your speed effectively first. Then it provides some speed-skill combination training to develop your ability to execute fine skills at high speeds.

See chapter 8 for advice on using intensity and getting the most out of your speed training. If you are unfamiliar with the specific speed drills used in the following workouts, turn to chapter 8 for an explanation. The combination speed-skill drills are also outlined in chapter 8.

Power and Quickness

Power and quickness are needed in hockey for starts and stops, for quick acceleration, for snap shots, for holding your position against opposition, for cutting, for turning, for footwork, and the list goes on. Almost all goaltenders' moves—blocking shots, kicking a puck away, or scrambling out of one position into another—require power and quickness. You can't play good hockey without power and quickness, no matter what position you play.

Power and quickness differ considerably from speed in that they are more explosive. They are super high intensity but can't be sustained as speed is. That's because the fuel for the extreme intensity comes from a simple chemical that is in limited supply right in the muscle cells. The fuel blasts fast, like dynamite, but then it is gone and must be replaced before another blast can occur. Training to improve power and quickness builds larger fuel stockpiles and greater provision for replacing fuel quickly so that the muscle is ready to go again.

Obviously, players need power and quickness in their upper-body muscles to shoot and fend off checkers. They also need power and quickness in the legs to start, stop, and deke. But training for quadriceps power does not give your biceps power. You must train each muscle group independently. So your training program must include power and quickness exercises for both upper- and lower-body muscles. The *52-Week* preseason program includes power and quickness exercises for all hockey muscle groups that need power.

As with speed training, intensity is the key to improving power and quickness. See chapter 9 for what constitutes effective intensity. Preseason power and quickness drills, like speed drills, begin off-ice so that you can develop a feel for the necessary intensity to create improvement. The drills then move predominately on-ice to gain the specificity that is critical for making power and quickness training transfer to hockey skills. Some power-quickness-skill combination exercises are provided to help players gain the ability to execute skills well at high speeds. For example, an accurate snap shot is much more deadly if a player can execute it on the fly or off a sudden change in direction. See chapter 9 for an explanation of the power and quickness drills and exercises used in the following workouts if they are unfamiliar to you.

By training for power and quickness in both upper- and lower-body muscle groups, you will have the means for executing explosive moves in a game.

Combination Fitness Training

At the outset of this chapter, we said that you had to maintain aerobics, muscle strength, muscle endurance, and flexibility throughout the preseason. Otherwise, you would lose your base, which would negatively affect both your ability to train and your skill performance.

Fortunately, you can do aerobic maintenance in combination with speed, power, and quickness training. Combination training permits efficient use of time in the preseason when coaches must work to improve many other aspects of the game. Combination training also has the benefit of being specific to game conditions because paces, durations, and length of rest periods vary throughout each shift and period of a game. This form of training is therefore an extremely useful tool in hockey training.

When you train speed, power, and quickness in combination with aerobics, intensity is still critical. Apply the principles outlined in chapter 7 regarding the perceived exertion scale and see chapters 8 and 9 for appropriate intensity guidelines. Practice these intensities in a nontraining situation first to get a good feel for what they are for you.

The *52-Week* program uses a five-level combination training program periodically throughout the preseason, as well as in-season, when practice and training time become overburdened with divergent demands. See table 2.1 for the combination fitness training program used in the *52-Week* program.

Post this program on the wall where you do your preseason workouts. If you have sufficient ice time, you can do the program on-ice. In that case, skate the perimeter of the ice for the easy and strong portions, use lines for the all-out portions, and use widths or the center and blue lines only for explosive portions. Be sure to reverse direction of perimeter skating and stops-turns so that you work turning in both directions.

Table 2.1 Combination Fitness Training Program

Level	Activity: running, cycling, cross-country skiing, skating
1	5 min easy, 30 min strong, 6-10 reps of 10 sec explosive: 50 sec easy
2	5 min easy, 30 min strong, 4-6 reps of 30 sec all out: 60 sec easy
3	5 min easy, 30 min strong, 4-8 reps of 30 sec all out: 45 sec easy
4	5 min easy, 30 min strong, 6-10 reps of 30 sec all out: 30 sec easy
5	5 min easy, 30 min strong, 3-4 reps of 10 sec explosive: 30 sec easy: 30 sec all out: 45 sec easy: 20 sec explosive: 45 sec easy

Combination Fitness-Skill Training

Some drills in the *52-Week* preseason training program combine work on the fitness elements of speed or power and quickness with specific hockey skills, like shooting and footwork. The purpose of these drills is to help apply your fitness improvements to your skills. For example, if you develop quick, powerful wrist action you want to be able to transfer that to executing an accurate snap shot on the fly. The fitness-skill combination drills help you perform skills more effectively. But there is one note of caution in using these drills. You should not rely exclusively on combination skill drills to maintain the fitness aspects of speed and power and quickness. It is extremely difficult to do combination skill drills at a sufficiently high intensity to improve or maintain high-level fitness standards. You must therefore periodically perform pure speed and power-quickness exercises to improve and maintain those aspects of your conditioning. The *52-Week* program uses both pure and combination skill drills in preseason and in-season.

The preseason workouts of the *52-Week* plan follow. A nine-week package provides a reasonable length of time for developing game-specific speed, power, and quickness. Remember that the workouts set ideal targets that you may have to adjust to suit your progress.

Note too that a schedule of preseason exhibition games is not included in the preseason workouts. Every team has a different exhibition schedule. Some games are considered important; some are not. If the team needs to be well rested for such games, do not do strength or speed work (alone or in combination) in the 48 hours before game time. Light aerobic and power-quickness work, along with flexibility training, are appropriate.

Preseason Workouts

Purpose
- To develop the fitness elements that maximize hockey performance
- To integrate the fitness elements in hockey skills
- To maintain the off-season fitness base

Focus
- Build speed, power, and quickness
- Move from general to specific training and apply to skills
- Maintain aerobic conditioning, muscle strength, muscle endurance, and flexibility

Reminders
- (30:30) = 30 seconds all out then 30 seconds (active) rest
- HRR = hold–relax–repeat
- 6-3-1 tempo = 6-second initial move–3-second hold–1-second return to start position
- 1 min at 1/sec = repeat one complete cycle of the exercise every second for 1 minute

Week 9 Preseason

	Program/activity	Sets/repetitions
MONDAY	**COMBINATION**	
	Level 1	6 reps
	SPEED	
	Off-ice short shift	(30:30) 6 reps
	FLEXIBILITY	
	Sequence program	2 × 20 sec HRR

	Program/activity	Sets/repetitions
TUESDAY	**COMBINATION**	
	Level 2	4 reps
	POWER AND QUICKNESS	
	Power push-ups I	6 reps, 2 sets
	Tuck jumps I	6 reps, 2 sets
	Lateral line jumps I	6 reps, 2 sets
	FLEXIBILITY	
	Sequence program	2 × 20 sec HRR

	Program/activity	Sets/repetitions
WEDNESDAY	**AEROBIC**	
	Select level 7, 8, or 9	
	STRENGTH	
	Unstable workout	3 sets, 6-8 reps, 6-3-1 tempo
	FLEXIBILITY	
	Sequence program	2 × 20 sec HRR

	Program/activity	Sets/repetitions
THURSDAY	**COMBINATION**	
	Level 1	6 reps
	SPEED	
	Off-ice long shift	(45:45) 4 reps
	FLEXIBILITY	
	Sequence program	2 × 20 sec HRR

PRESEASON

	Program/activity	Sets/repetitions
FRIDAY	**COMBINATION**	
	Level 3	4 reps
	POWER AND QUICKNESS	
	Power push-ups I	8 reps, 2 sets
	Tuck jumps I	8 reps, 2 sets
	Lateral line jumps I	8 reps, 2 sets
	FLEXIBILITY	
	Sequence program	2 × 20 sec HRR

SATURDAY	**AEROBIC**	
	Select level 7, 8, or 9	
	STRENGTH	
	Core program	3 sets, 4-6 reps, 2-1-2 tempo
	MUSCLE ENDURANCE	
	Core program	1 set, 1 min at 1/sec
	FLEXIBILITY	
	Sequence program	2 × 20 sec HRR

SUN	**DAY OFF**

Week 10 Preseason

MONDAY

Program/activity	Sets/repetitions
COMBINATION	
Level 1	8 reps
SPEED	
Off-ice ladder drill	4 reps
FLEXIBILITY	
Sequence program	2 × 20 sec HRR

TUESDAY

Program/activity	Sets/repetitions
COMBINATION	
Level 2	6 reps
POWER AND QUICKNESS	
Power push-ups I	8 reps, 2 sets
Tuck jumps I	8 reps, 2 sets
Lateral line jumps I	8 reps, 2 sets
FLEXIBILITY	
Sequence program	2 × 20 sec HRR

WEDNESDAY

Program/activity	Sets/repetitions
AEROBIC	
Select level 7, 8, or 9	
STRENGTH	
Unstable workout	3 sets, 6-8 reps, 6-3-1 tempo
FLEXIBILITY	
Sequence program	2 × 20 sec HRR

THURSDAY

Program/activity	Sets/repetitions
COMBINATION	
Level 1	8 reps
SPEED	
Off-ice ladder drill	5 reps
FLEXIBILITY	
Sequence program	2 × 20 sec HRR

	Program/activity	Sets/repetitions
FRIDAY	**COMBINATION**	
	Level 3	6 reps
	POWER AND QUICKNESS	
	Power push-ups II	4 reps, 2 sets
	Tuck jumps II	4 reps, 2 sets
	Lateral line jumps II	4 reps, 2 sets
	FLEXIBILITY	
	Sequence program	2 × 20 sec HRR

SATURDAY	**AEROBIC**	
	Select level 7, 8, or 9	
	STRENGTH	
	Core program	3 sets, 4-6 reps, 2-1-2 tempo
	MUSCLE ENDURANCE	
	Core program	1 set, 1 min at 1/sec
	FLEXIBILITY	
	Sequence program	2 × 20 sec HRR

SUN	**DAY OFF**

Week 11 Preseason

<table>
<tr><td rowspan="6">MONDAY</td><td>Program/activity</td><td>Sets/repetitions</td></tr>
<tr><td>COMBINATION</td><td></td></tr>
<tr><td>Level 1</td><td>10 reps</td></tr>
<tr><td>SPEED</td><td></td></tr>
<tr><td>Off-ice short shift</td><td>(30:30) 8 reps</td></tr>
<tr><td>FLEXIBILITY</td><td></td></tr>
</table>

MONDAY	Program/activity	Sets/repetitions
	COMBINATION	
	Level 1	10 reps
	SPEED	
	Off-ice short shift	(30:30) 8 reps
	FLEXIBILITY	
	Sequence program	2 × 20 sec HRR

TUESDAY		
	COMBINATION	
	Level 3	8 reps
	POWER AND QUICKNESS	
	Power push-ups II	6 reps, 2 sets
	Tuck jumps II	6 reps, 2 sets
	Lateral line jumps II	6 reps, 2 sets
	FLEXIBILITY	
	Sequence program	2 × 20 sec HRR

WEDNESDAY		
	AEROBIC	
	Select level 7, 8, or 9	
	STRENGTH	
	Unstable workout	3 sets, 6-8 reps, 6-3-1 tempo
	FLEXIBILITY	
	Sequence program	2 × 20 sec HRR

THURSDAY		
	COMBINATION	
	Level 1	10 reps
	SPEED	
	Off-ice long shift	(45:45) 6 reps
	FLEXIBILITY	
	Sequence program	2 × 20 sec HRR

Program/activity	Sets/repetitions
FRIDAY	
COMBINATION	
Level 4	6 reps
POWER AND QUICKNESS	
Power push-ups II	8 reps, 2 sets
Tuck jumps II	8 reps, 2 sets
Lateral line jumps II	8 reps, 2 sets
FLEXIBILITY	
Sequence program	2 × 20 sec HRR

Program/activity	Sets/repetitions
SATURDAY	
AEROBIC	
Select level 7, 8, or 9	
STRENGTH	
Core program	3 sets, 4-6 reps, 2-1-2 tempo
MUSCLE ENDURANCE	
Core program	1 set, 1 min at 1/sec
FLEXIBILITY	
Sequence program	2 × 20 sec HRR

SUN	**DAY OFF**

Week 12 Preseason

	Program/activity	Sets/repetitions
MONDAY	**AEROBIC**	
	Level 9	
	POWER AND QUICKNESS	
	Incline blast	(10:50) 6 reps, 2 sets
	Arm step-ups	(10:50) 6 reps, 2 sets
	SPEED	
	Off-ice ladder drill	6 reps
	FLEXIBILITY	
	Sequence program	2 × 20 sec HRR

	Program/activity	Sets/repetitions
TUESDAY	**COMBINATION**	
	Level 4	8 reps
	POWER AND QUICKNESS	
	Power push-ups II	8 reps, 2 sets
	Tuck jumps II	8 reps, 2 sets
	Lateral line jumps II	8 reps, 2 sets
	FLEXIBILITY	
	Sequence program	2 × 20 sec HRR

	Program/activity	Sets/repetitions
WEDNESDAY	**AEROBIC**	
	Select level 7 or 8	
	STRENGTH	
	Unstable workout	3 sets, 6-8 reps, 6-3-1 tempo
	FLEXIBILITY	
	Sequence program	2 × 20 sec HRR

	Program/activity	Sets/repetitions
THURSDAY	**AEROBIC**	
	Level 9	
	POWER AND QUICKNESS	
	Incline blast	(10:50) 8 reps, 2 sets
	Arm step-ups	(10:50) 8 reps, 2 sets
	SPEED	
	Off-ice ladder drill	7 reps
	FLEXIBILITY	
	Sequence program	2 × 20 sec HRR

FRIDAY	**COMBINATION**	
	Level 4	10 reps
	POWER AND QUICKNESS	
	Power push-ups II	8 reps, 2 sets
	Tuck jumps II	8 reps, 2 sets
	Lateral line jumps II	8 reps, 2 sets
	FLEXIBILITY	
	Sequence program	2 × 20 sec HRR

SATURDAY	**AEROBIC**	
	Select level 7 or 8	
	STRENGTH	
	Core program	3 sets, 4-6 reps, 2-1-2 tempo
	MUSCLE ENDURANCE	
	Core program	1 set, 1 min at 1/sec
	FLEXIBILITY	
	Sequence program	2 × 20 sec HRR

SUN	**DAY OFF**	

Week 13 Preseason

MONDAY

Program/activity	Sets/repetitions
AEROBIC	
Level 9	
POWER AND QUICKNESS	
Off-ice: incline blast	(10:50) 10 reps, 2 sets
Arm step-ups	(10:50) 10 reps, 2 sets
SPEED	
On-ice short shift	(30:30) 6 reps
FLEXIBILITY	
Sequence program	2 × 20 sec HRR

TUESDAY

Program/activity	Sets/repetitions
STRENGTH	
Unstable workout	3 sets, 6-8 reps, 8-2-4 tempo
MUSCLE ENDURANCE	
Core program	1 set, 1 min at 1/sec
POWER AND QUICKNESS	
Puck bash	6 reps at 10 feet
Circle shuttle	(10:50) 6 reps
FLEXIBILITY	
Sequence program	2 × 20 sec HRR

WEDNESDAY

Program/activity	Sets/repetitions
AEROBIC	
Level 9	
POWER AND QUICKNESS	
Quick-release drill	6 reps
SPEED	
On-ice short shift	(30:30) 8 reps
FLEXIBILITY	
Sequence program	2 × 20 sec HRR

	Program/activity	Sets/repetitions
THURSDAY	**POWER AND QUICKNESS**	
	Puck bash	8 reps at 10 feet
	Center shuttle	On 1 min, 6 reps
	FLEXIBILITY	
	Sequence program	2 × 20 sec HRR

FRIDAY	**AEROBIC**	
	Level 9	
	POWER AND QUICKNESS	
	Off-ice: incline blast	(10:50) 12 reps, 2 sets
	Arm step-ups	(10:50) 12 reps, 2 sets
	SPEED	
	Skaters—on-ice long shift	(45:45) 4 reps
	POWER AND QUICKNESS	
	Goalies—scramble drill	(10:50) 6 reps
	FLEXIBILITY	
	Sequence program	2 × 20 sec HRR

SATURDAY	**STRENGTH**	
	Core program	3 sets, 4-6 reps, 2-1-2 tempo
	POWER AND QUICKNESS	
	Power push-ups II	8 reps, 2 sets
	Tuck jumps II	8 reps, 2 sets
	Lateral line jumps II	8 reps, 2 sets
	FLEXIBILITY	
	Sequence program	2 × 20 sec HRR

SUN	**DAY OFF**	

Week 14 Preseason

	Program/activity	Sets/repetitions
MONDAY	**STRENGTH**	
	Core program	3 sets, 4-6 reps, 2-1-2 tempo
	POWER AND QUICKNESS	
	Puck bash	10 reps at 10 feet
	Circle shuttle	(10:50) 8 reps
	FLEXIBILITY	
	Sequence program	2 × 20 sec HRR

	Program/activity	Sets/repetitions
TUESDAY	**AEROBIC**	
	Level 9	
	MUSCLE ENDURANCE	
	Core program	1 set, 1 min at 1/sec
	SPEED	
	On-ice line ladder drill	4 reps
	FLEXIBILITY	
	Sequence program	2 × 20 sec HRR

	Program/activity	Sets/repetitions
WEDNESDAY	**AEROBIC**	
	Select level 7 or 8	
	STRENGTH	
	Unstable workout	3 sets, 6-8 reps, 8-2-4 tempo
	POWER AND QUICKNESS	
	Figure-8 pass drill	6 reps (include goalies)
	Quick-shot drill	6 reps (goalies in net)
	FLEXIBILITY	
	Sequence program	2 × 20 sec HRR

Program/activity	Sets/repetitions
THURSDAY	
AEROBIC	
Level 9	
SPEED	
On-ice line ladder drill	5 reps
FLEXIBILITY	
Sequence program	2 × 20 sec HRR

Program/activity	Sets/repetitions
FRIDAY	
SPEED	
Skaters—3-on-2 in-the-zone drill	4 reps
POWER AND QUICKNESS	
Goalies—telescoping	6 reps
FLEXIBILITY	
Sequence program	2 × 20 sec HRR

Program/activity	Sets/repetitions
SATURDAY	
STRENGTH	
Core program	3 sets, 4-6 reps, 2-1-2 tempo
POWER AND QUICKNESS	
Off-ice: incline blast	(10:50) 12 reps, 2 sets
Arm step-ups	(10:50) 12 reps, 2 sets
FLEXIBILITY	
Sequence program	2 × 20 sec HRR

SUN	**DAY OFF**

Week 15 Preseason

	Program/activity	Sets/repetitions
MONDAY	**SPEED**	
	On-ice short shift	(30:30) 8 reps
	FLEXIBILITY	
	Sequence program	2 × 20 sec HRR

	Program/activity	Sets/repetitions
TUESDAY	**COMBINATION**	
	Level 5	2 reps
	POWER AND QUICKNESS	
	Puck bash	6 reps at 15 feet
	Circle shuttle	(10:50) 10 reps
	FLEXIBILITY	
	Sequence program	2 × 20 sec HRR

	Program/activity	Sets/repetitions
WEDNESDAY	**SPEED**	
	Skaters—3-on-3 cross-zone drill	6 reps
	POWER AND QUICKNESS	
	Goalies—scramble drill	(10:50) 10 reps
	FLEXIBILITY	
	Sequence program	2 × 20 sec HRR

	Program/activity	Sets/repetitions
THURSDAY	**AEROBIC**	
	Level 9	
	MUSCLE ENDURANCE	
	Core program	1 set, 1 min at 1/sec
	POWER AND QUICKNESS	
	Skaters—your shot drill	6 reps
	Goalies—lateral-movement drill	6 reps
	FLEXIBILITY	
	Sequence program	2 × 20 sec HRR

Program/activity	Sets/repetitions
FRIDAY	
SPEED	
Skaters—on-ice line ladder drill	6 reps
Goalies—five-point shooting	4 reps
FLEXIBILITY	
Sequence program	2 × 20 sec HRR

Program/activity	Sets/repetitions
SATURDAY	
COMBINATION	
Level 5	3 reps
STRENGTH	
Core program	3 sets, 4-6 reps, 2-1-2 tempo
POWER AND QUICKNESS	
Power push-ups II	10 reps, 2 sets
Tuck jumps II	10 reps, 2 sets
Lateral line jumps II	10 reps, 2 sets
FLEXIBILITY	
Sequence program	2 × 20 sec HRR

SUN	**DAY OFF**

Week 16 Preseason

MONDAY

Program/activity	Sets/repetitions
SPEED	
On-ice short shift	(30:30) 10 reps
POWER AND QUICKNESS	
Puck bash	8 reps at 15 feet
Circle shuttle	(10:30) 12 reps
FLEXIBILITY	
Sequence program	2 × 20 sec HRR

TUESDAY

SPEED	
Forwards and defense—3-on-2 switch drill	4 reps
POWER AND QUICKNESS	
Goalies—down-up shot drill	6 reps
Forwards—quick-corner drill	8 reps
Defense—walk-and-shoot drill	8 reps
FLEXIBILITY	
Sequence program	2 × 20 sec HRR

WEDNESDAY

AEROBIC	
Level 9	
POWER AND QUICKNESS	
Incline blast	(10:50) 12 reps, 2 sets
Arm step-ups	(10:50) 12 reps, 2 sets
FLEXIBILITY	
Sequence program	2 × 20 sec HRR

Program/activity	Sets/repetitions
THURSDAY	
SPEED	
Skaters—on-ice long shift	(45:45) 6 reps
POWER AND QUICKNESS	
Goalies—down-ups	(10:50) 8 reps
Forwards—shooting drill	8 reps
Defense—1-on-1 quick-up drill	8 reps
FLEXIBILITY	
Sequence program	2 × 20 sec HRR

Program/activity	Sets/repetitions
FRIDAY	
SPEED	
Line ladder drill	8 reps
POWER AND QUICKNESS	
Skaters—puck bash	8 reps at 20 feet
Center shuttle	On 45 sec, 6 reps
Goalies—wraparound drill	6 reps
FLEXIBILITY	
Sequence program	2 × 20 sec HRR

Program/activity	Sets/repetitions
SATURDAY	
COMBINATION	
Level 5	4 reps
STRENGTH	
Core program	3 sets, 4-6 reps, 2-1-2 tempo
POWER AND QUICKNESS	
Power push-ups II	12 reps, 2 sets
Tuck jumps II	12 reps, 2 sets
Lateral line jumps II	12 reps, 2 sets
FLEXIBILITY	
Sequence program	2 × 20 sec HRR

SUN	**DAY OFF**

Week 17 Preseason

MONDAY

Program/activity	Sets/repetitions
SPEED	
Forwards—attack drill	4 reps
Defense—get-out drill	4 reps
POWER AND QUICKNESS	
Puck bash	10 reps at 20 feet
Circle shuttle	(10:30) 8 reps
FLEXIBILITY	
Sequence program	2 × 20 sec HRR

TUESDAY

Program/activity	Sets/repetitions
SPEED	
Skaters—continuous scrimmage	6 reps
POWER AND QUICKNESS	
Goalies—scramble drill	(10:50) 12 reps
Skaters—your shot drill	8 reps
Goalies—telescoping	8 reps
FLEXIBILITY	
Sequence program	2 × 20 sec HRR

WEDNESDAY

Program/activity	Sets/repetitions
COMBINATION	
Level 5	4 reps
STRENGTH	
Unstable workout	3 sets, 6-8 reps, 8-2-4 tempo
POWER AND QUICKNESS	
Incline blast	(10:50) 12 reps, 2 sets
Arm step-ups	(10:50) 12 reps, 2 sets
FLEXIBILITY	
Sequence program	2 × 20 sec HRR

	Program/activity	Sets/repetitions
THURSDAY	**SPEED**	
	Skaters—on-ice long shift	(45:45) 8 reps
	Goalies—five-point shooting	6 reps
	POWER AND QUICKNESS	
	Skaters—puck bash	12 reps at 20 feet
	Center shuttle	On 45 sec, 8 reps
	Goalies—lateral-movement drill	8 reps
	FLEXIBILITY	
	Sequence program	2 × 20 sec HRR

FRI	**DAY OFF**

SAT	**DAY OFF**

SUN	**DAY OFF**

Chapter
3

In-Season Workouts

"Luck is what happens when preparation meets opportunity."—**Darrel Royal**

Now comes your opportunity. The games begin. If you prepared well, you will play well. If your team has prepared well, luck will be on your side. You have what it takes to make it happen.

All you have to do now for conditioning is keep what you built. Maintain your aerobic, muscle strength, muscle endurance, and flexibility base. Ease into maintenance of your speed, power, and quickness. Maintenance training doesn't take a lot of time, but it does take specific effort. Remember, games don't keep you in shape. You sit far too much during a game for it to benefit your strength, endurance, aerobics, speed, power, quickness, and flexibility. In addition, the intensity of effort and the length and frequency of rest intervals that are part of the game don't meet the requirements of a training session for any aspect of fitness.

The conditioning workouts for the *52-Week* in-season program are designed to give you maximum maintenance benefit in a minimum amount of time so that you can spend most of your in-season practice time on skill work and game preparation. One way of maximizing training time is to do combination training. To that end, in the in-season you regularly use the combination fitness drills and combination fitness-skill drills that you began to use in the preseason. Pure training sessions are interjected when timing is appropriate to ensure that the fitness element is not being compromised. For example, if forwards rely exclusively on quickness-shooting drills for combination training throughout the in-season, their shooting power will likely decline more than if they include a pure power-quickness training session like arm step-ups every other week. By using combination training sessions and pure training sessions throughout the playing season, players can maintain the high level of fitness they established in the off-season and preseason.

You've prepared your body for the work of playing the game, but you must still maintain your level of fitness by training during the in-season.

One difficulty with trying to present daily in-season workouts for all hockey teams is that teams play vastly different game schedules. Some teams play a 20-week league schedule; others play 30-week seasons. Some teams play one or two games a week, only on weekends; others play three or four games a week spread throughout the week. Some teams don't lose much time on travel days; other teams may lose two or more days a week to travel. These time constraints affect the scheduling of practice and training sessions.

To provide in-season conditioning programs that could work for the widest variety of elite-level hockey players, *52-Week Hockey Training* divides the in-season into four blocks, lettered A, B, C, and D, each six weeks long. Each block represents a different type of scheduling. A fifth block (E) represents a typical playoff schedule. See table 3.1 to identify which block best suits your game schedule and training needs.

Note the week numbers used in the block that best represents your team's schedule. Turn to those week numbers in the workouts to find the daily plans for your in-season training. Repeat that block of training weeks for the duration of your in-season training schedule. This approach will ensure that you train muscle strength, muscle endurance, aerobics, flexibility, speed, power, and quickness frequently enough to maintain the high level of fitness you had at the start of the playing season.

You may find that you have to adjust the block to suit your game schedule better. Apply the following principles in making your modifications.

Table 3.1 In-Season Training Blocks

Block	Use weeks	If your schedule is	Example
A	18–23	1-2 games/week, primarily weekends	College, tournament play
B	24–29	1-2 games/week, weekdays and weekends	Minor hockey
C	30–35	1-3 games/week, weekdays and weekends	Junior hockey
D	36–41	1-4 games/week plus travel days lost	Professional hockey
E	42–48	Playoffs, some weekday games*	

*If your playoffs are weekend games only or tournaments, use the block of weeks 18–23.

1. Do not train strength or speed (or combination speed work) in the 48 hours before a game.
2. Do flexibility work following every practice.
3. Use medium-level aerobic work to help refresh your muscles and cardiovascular system the day after a hard workout or game.
4. You should usually do speed and power-quickness work on-ice. Off-ice work should be used occasionally (every two or three weeks) to do a pure training session.
5. If you are typically in block C or D but have a week with only one game, take advantage of the time to top up your aerobics, muscle strength, muscle endurance, and speed. These fundamentals take a beating during heavy game schedules.
6. If game and travel schedules render training time almost negligible over a two-week period, do at least two aerobics and three power-quickness sessions during that period besides daily flexibility work.

Regardless of which training block you use, you will notice that the in-season *52-Week* workout schedule often lists a flexibility workout on days before or between games. On those days, workouts are often optional, and later in the season, they are days off. Do the flexibility work if you have a light practice; if not, relax.

As time becomes more of a premium in-season, you may find it more convenient to do your aerobic and combination fitness training on a stationary bike at the rink, rather than at an outdoor course. If weather permits, an occasional run or cross-country ski session would be of benefit. Remember that water running is a good choice for aerobic or combination work if seasonal wear and tear is taking its toll.

The following are your in-season workouts. Draw lots of luck your way this season.

In-Season Workouts

Purpose
- To maintain the high level of fitness established by off-season and preseason training

Focus
- Maintain aerobics, muscle strength, muscle endurance, speed, power, quickness, and flexibility

Reminders
- (10:50) = 10 seconds at explosive pace then 50 seconds (active) rest
- HRR = hold–relax–repeat
- 2-1-2 tempo = 2-second initial move–1-second hold–2-second return to start position
- 1 min at 1/sec = repeat one complete cycle of the exercise every second for 1 minute

Week 18 In-Season Block A

MONDAY

Program/activity	Sets/repetitions
STRENGTH	
Core program	2 sets, 4-6 reps
Unstable workout	1 set, 6-8 reps, all 2-1-2 tempo
POWER AND QUICKNESS	
Skaters—slot drill	(10:50) 6 reps
Goalies—scramble drill	(10:50) 10 reps
Everyone—circle shuttle	(10:50) 10 reps
FLEXIBILITY	
Sequence program	1 × 10-20 sec HRR

TUESDAY

Program/activity	Sets/repetitions
COMBINATION	
Level 5	4 reps
MUSCLE ENDURANCE	
Core program	1 set, 1 min at 1/sec
FLEXIBILITY	
Sequence program	1 × 10-20 sec HRR

WEDNESDAY

Program/activity	Sets/repetitions
AEROBIC	
Select level 7, 8, or 9	
POWER AND QUICKNESS	
Forwards—shooting drill	8 reps
Defense—1-on-1 quick-up drill	8 reps
Goalies—wraparound drill	8 reps
FLEXIBILITY	
Sequence program	1 × 10-20 sec HRR

THURS

Program/activity	Sets/repetitions
FLEXIBILITY	
Sequence program	1 × 10-20 sec HRR

FRI	GAME	

SAT	GAME	

SUN	DAY OFF	

Week 19 In-Season Block A

	Program/activity	Sets/repetitions
MONDAY	**STRENGTH**	
	Core program	2 sets, 4-6 reps
	Unstable workout	1 set, 6-8 reps, all 2-1-2 tempo
	POWER AND QUICKNESS	
	Skaters—figure-8 pass drill	8 reps
	Goalies—lateral-movement drill	10 reps
	FLEXIBILITY	
	Sequence program	1 × 10-20 sec HRR

	Program/activity	Sets/repetitions
TUESDAY	**COMBINATION**	
	Level 1	8 reps
	SPEED	
	Line ladder drill	6 reps
	FLEXIBILITY	
	Sequence program	1 × 10-20 sec HRR

IN-SEASON

Program/activity	Sets/repetitions
WEDNESDAY	
AEROBIC	
Select level 7, 8, or 9	
POWER AND QUICKNESS	
Puck bash	12 reps at 10 feet
Circle shuttle	(10:30) 10 reps
FLEXIBILITY	
Sequence program	1 × 10-20 sec HRR

THURS	
FLEXIBILITY	
Sequence program	1 × 10-20 sec HRR

FRI	
GAME	

SAT	
FLEXIBILITY	
Sequence program	1 × 10-20 sec HRR

SUN	
GAME	

IN-SEASON

Week 20 In-Season Block A

	Program/activity	Sets/repetitions
MON	**DAY OFF**	

	Program/activity	Sets/repetitions
TUESDAY	**STRENGTH**	
	Core program	2 sets, 4-6 reps
	Unstable workout	1 set, 6-8 reps, all 2-1-2 tempo
	POWER AND QUICKNESS	
	Skaters—slot drill	(10:50) 10 reps
	Goalies—down-ups	(10:50) 8 reps
	Everyone—center shuttle	On 45 sec, 8 reps
	FLEXIBILITY	
	Sequence program	1 × 10-20 sec HRR

	Program/activity	Sets/repetitions
WEDNESDAY	**COMBINATION**	
	Level 5	4 reps
	MUSCLE ENDURANCE	
	Core program	1 set, 1 min at 1/sec
	FLEXIBILITY	
	Sequence program	1 × 10-20 sec HRR

	Program/activity	Sets/repetitions
THURSDAY	**AEROBIC**	
	Select level 7, 8, or 9	
	POWER AND QUICKNESS	
	Puck bash	12 reps at 15 feet
	Circle shuttle	(10:50) 10 reps
	FLEXIBILITY	
	Sequence program	1 × 10-20 sec HRR

IN-SEASON

	Program/activity	Sets/repetitions
FRI	**FLEXIBILITY**	
	Sequence program	1 × 10-20 sec HRR

SAT	**GAME**

SUN	**GAME**

Week 21 In-Season Block A

	Program/activity	Sets/repetitions
MON	**DAY OFF**	

TUESDAY	**STRENGTH**	
	Core program	2 sets, 4-6 reps
	Unstable workout	1 set, 6-8 reps, all 2-1-2 tempo
	POWER AND QUICKNESS	
	Skaters—quick-release drill	8 reps
	Goalies—down-up shot drill	8 reps
	FLEXIBILITY	
	Sequence program	1 × 10-20 sec HRR

WEDNESDAY	**COMBINATION**	
	Level 1	10 reps
	SPEED	
	Skaters—continuous scrimmage	8 reps
	Goalies—five-point shooting	8 reps
	FLEXIBILITY	
	Sequence program	1 × 10-20 sec HRR

	THURS
FLEXIBILITY	
Sequence program	1 × 10-20 sec HRR

	FRI
GAME	

	SAT
GAME	

	SUN
DAY OFF	

Week 22 In-Season Block A

	Program/activity	Sets/repetitions
MONDAY	**STRENGTH**	
	Core program	2 sets, 4-6 reps
	Unstable workout	1 set, 6-8 reps, all 2-1-2 tempo
	POWER AND QUICKNESS	
	Skaters—slot drill	(15:45) 10 reps
	Goalies—scramble drill	(10:50) 10 reps
	Everyone—circle shuttle	(10:30) 10 reps
	FLEXIBILITY	
	Sequence program	1 × 10-20 sec HRR

	COMBINATION	
TUESDAY	Level 4	8 reps
	POWER AND QUICKNESS	
	Incline blast	(10:50) 10 reps, 2 sets
	Arm step-ups	(10:50) 10 reps, 2 sets
	FLEXIBILITY	
	Sequence program	1 × 10-20 sec HRR

Program/activity	Sets/repetitions
WEDNESDAY	
COMBINATION	
Level 1	10 reps
SPEED	
Skaters—on-ice long shift	(45:45) 6 reps
POWER AND QUICKNESS	
Goalies—down-ups	(10:50) 10 reps
FLEXIBILITY	
Sequence program	1 × 10-20 sec HRR

Program/activity	Sets/repetitions
THURSDAY	
AEROBIC	
Select level 7, 8, or 9	
POWER AND QUICKNESS	
Skaters—quick-shot drill	8 reps
Goalies—wraparound drill	10 reps
FLEXIBILITY	
Sequence program	1 × 10-20 sec HRR

FRI	
FLEXIBILITY	
Sequence program	1 × 10-20 sec HRR

SAT	**GAME**

SUN	**DAY OFF**

Week 23 In-Season Block A

<table>
<tr><th></th><th>Program/activity</th><th>Sets/repetitions</th></tr>
<tr><td rowspan="8">MONDAY</td><td colspan="2">STRENGTH</td></tr>
<tr><td>Core program</td><td>2 sets, 4-6 reps</td></tr>
<tr><td>Unstable workout</td><td>1 set, 6-8 reps, all 2-1-2 tempo</td></tr>
<tr><td colspan="2">POWER AND QUICKNESS</td></tr>
<tr><td>Skaters—your shot drill</td><td>10 reps</td></tr>
<tr><td>Goalies—telescoping</td><td>10 reps</td></tr>
<tr><td colspan="2">FLEXIBILITY</td></tr>
<tr><td>Sequence program</td><td>1 × 10-20 sec HRR</td></tr>
</table>

<table>
<tr><td rowspan="6">TUESDAY</td><td colspan="2">COMBINATION</td></tr>
<tr><td>Level 1</td><td>10 reps</td></tr>
<tr><td colspan="2">SPEED</td></tr>
<tr><td>3-on-2 switch drill</td><td>6 reps</td></tr>
<tr><td colspan="2">FLEXIBILITY</td></tr>
<tr><td>Sequence program</td><td>1 × 10-20 sec HRR</td></tr>
</table>

<table>
<tr><td rowspan="7">WEDNESDAY</td><td colspan="2">AEROBIC</td></tr>
<tr><td colspan="2">Select level 7, 8, or 9</td></tr>
<tr><td colspan="2">POWER AND QUICKNESS</td></tr>
<tr><td>Puck bash</td><td>12 reps at 20 feet</td></tr>
<tr><td>Circle shuttle</td><td>(10:50) 10 reps</td></tr>
<tr><td colspan="2">FLEXIBILITY</td></tr>
<tr><td>Sequence program</td><td>1 × 10-20 sec HRR</td></tr>
</table>

<table>
<tr><td rowspan="2">THURS</td><td colspan="2">FLEXIBILITY</td></tr>
<tr><td>Sequence program</td><td>1 × 10-20 sec HRR</td></tr>
</table>

	Program/activity	Sets/repetitions
FRI	GAME	

	Program/activity	Sets/repetitions
SAT	GAME	

	Program/activity	Sets/repetitions
SUN	GAME	

Week 24 In-Season Block B

	Program/activity	Sets/repetitions
MONDAY	**AEROBIC**	
	Level 7	
	POWER AND QUICKNESS	
	Skaters—quick-release drill	8 reps
	Goalies—wraparound drill	8 reps
	FLEXIBILITY	
	Sequence program	1 × 10-20 sec HRR

	Program/activity	Sets/repetitions
TUES	GAME	

	Program/activity	Sets/repetitions
WEDNESDAY	**STRENGTH**	
	Core program	2 sets, 4-6 reps
	Unstable workout	1 set, 6-8 reps, all 2-1-2 tempo
	POWER AND QUICKNESS	
	Skaters—slot drill	(10:50) 6 reps
	Goalies—scramble drill	(10:50) 6 reps
	Everyone—circle shuttle	(10:50) 8 reps
	FLEXIBILITY	
	Sequence program	1 × 10-20 sec HRR

THURSDAY	COMBINATION	
	Level 4	6 reps
	FLEXIBILITY	
	Sequence program	1 × 10-20 sec HRR

FRI	FLEXIBILITY	
	Sequence program	1 × 10-20 sec HRR

SAT	GAME	

SUN	DAY OFF	

Week 25 In-Season Block B

	Program/activity	Sets/repetitions
MONDAY	STRENGTH	
	Core program	2 sets, 4-6 reps
	Unstable workout	1 set, 6-8 reps, all 2-1-2 tempo
	MUSCLE ENDURANCE	
	Core program	1 set, 1 min at 1/sec
	AEROBIC	
	Select level 7, 8, or 9	
	FLEXIBILITY	
	Sequence program	1 × 10-20 sec HRR

TUESDAY	SPEED	
	Line ladder drill	8 reps
	FLEXIBILITY	
	Sequence program	1 × 10-20 sec HRR

	Program/activity	Sets/repetitions
WEDNESDAY	**AEROBIC**	
	Select level 7, 8, or 9	
	POWER AND QUICKNESS	
	Puck bash	8 reps at 15 feet
	Circle shuttle	(10:30) 8 reps
	FLEXIBILITY	
	Sequence program	1 × 10-20 sec HRR

THURS	**FLEXIBILITY**	
	Sequence program	1 × 10-20 sec HRR

FRI	**GAME**	

SAT	**GAME**	

SUN	**GAME**	

Week 26 In-Season Block B

	Program/activity	Sets/repetitions
MONDAY	**STRENGTH**	
	Core program	2 sets, 4-6 reps
	Unstable workout	1 set, 6-8 reps, all 2-1-2 tempo
	MUSCLE ENDURANCE	
	Core program	1 set, 1 min at 1/sec
	FLEXIBILITY	
	Sequence program	1 × 10-20 sec HRR

TUESDAY	COMBINATION	
	Level 4	8 reps
	POWER AND QUICKNESS	
	Skaters—your shot drill	10 reps
	Goalies—telescoping	10 reps
	FLEXIBILITY	
	Sequence program	1 × 10-20 sec HRR

WED	SPEED	
	On-ice short shift	(30:30) 10 reps
	FLEXIBILITY	
	Sequence program	1 × 10-20 sec HRR

THURSDAY	AEROBIC	
	Select level 7, 8, or 9	
	POWER AND QUICKNESS	
	Skaters—quick-shot drill	8 reps
	Goalies—down-up shot drill	8 reps
	FLEXIBILITY	
	Sequence program	1 × 10-20 sec HRR

FRI	FLEXIBILITY	
	Sequence program	1 × 10-20 sec HRR

SAT	GAME

SUN	GAME

IN-SEASON

Week 27 In-Season Block B

	Program/activity	Sets/repetitions
MON	**DAY OFF**	

	Program/activity	Sets/repetitions
TUESDAY	**STRENGTH**	
	Core program	2 sets, 4-6 reps
	Unstable workout	1 set, 6-8 reps, all 2-1-2 tempo
	POWER AND QUICKNESS	
	Skaters—slot drill	(10:50) 10 reps
	Goalies—down-ups	(10:50) 8 reps
	Everyone—center shuttle	On 1 min, 10 reps
	FLEXIBILITY	
	Sequence program	1 × 10-20 sec HRR

	Program/activity	Sets/repetitions
WEDNESDAY	**AEROBIC**	
	Select level 7, 8, or 9	
	SPEED	
	Forwards—challenge drill	6 reps
	Defense—net drill	6 reps
	Goalies—five-point shooting	8 reps
	FLEXIBILITY	
	Sequence program	1 × 10-20 sec HRR

	Program/activity	Sets/repetitions
THURSDAY	**POWER AND QUICKNESS**	
	Puck bash	8 reps at 20 feet
	Circle shuttle	(10:30) 8 reps
	FLEXIBILITY	
	Sequence program	1 × 10-20 sec HRR

	Program/activity	Sets/repetitions
FRI	**GAME**	

SAT	**FLEXIBILITY**	
	Sequence program	1 × 10-20 sec HRR

SUN	**GAME**	

Week 28 In-Season Block B

	Program/activity	Sets/repetitions
MON	**DAY OFF**	

TUESDAY	**POWER AND QUICKNESS**	
	Puck bash	8 reps at 15 feet
	Circle shuttle	(10:50) 8 reps
	FLEXIBILITY	
	Sequence program	1 × 10-20 sec HRR

WED	**GAME**	

THURSDAY	**AEROBIC**	
	Select level 7, 8, or 9	
	POWER AND QUICKNESS	
	Skaters—slot drill	(15:45) 8 reps
	Goalies—scramble drill	(10:50) 8 reps
	Everyone—center shuttle	On 45 sec, 8 reps
	FLEXIBILITY	
	Sequence program	1 × 10-20 sec HRR

	Program/activity	Sets/repetitions
FRI	**FLEXIBILITY**	
	Sequence program	1 × 10-20 sec HRR

SAT	**GAME**

SUN	**DAY OFF**

Week 29 In-Season Block B

	Program/activity	Sets/repetitions
MONDAY	**STRENGTH**	
	Core program	2 sets, 4-6 reps
	Unstable workout	1 set, 6-8 reps, all 2-1-2 tempo
	POWER AND QUICKNESS	
	Incline blast	(10:50) 10 reps, 2 sets
	Arm step-ups	(10:50) 10 reps, 2 sets
	FLEXIBILITY	
	Sequence program	1 × 10-20 sec HRR

	Program/activity	Sets/repetitions
TUESDAY	**COMBINATION**	
	Level 4	8 reps
	MUSCLE ENDURANCE	
	Core program	1 set, 1 min at 1/sec
	FLEXIBILITY	
	Sequence program	1 × 10-20 sec HRR

WEDNESDAY	**AEROBIC**	
	Select level 7, 8, or 9	
	SPEED	
	Skaters—long shift	(45:45) 8 reps
	POWER AND QUICKNESS	
	Goalies—lateral-movement drill	8 reps
	FLEXIBILITY	
	Sequence program	1 × 10-20 sec HRR

THURSDAY	**POWER AND QUICKNESS**	
	Puck bash	8 reps at 20 feet
	Circle shuttle	(10:50) 8 reps
	FLEXIBILITY	
	Sequence program	1 × 10-20 sec HRR

| FRI | **GAME** | |

SATURDAY	**STRENGTH**	
	Core program	2 sets, 4-6 reps
	Unstable workout	1 set, 6-8 reps, all 2-1-2 tempo
	AEROBIC	
	Level 9	
	FLEXIBILITY	
	Sequence program	1 × 10-20 sec HRR

| SUN | **DAY OFF** | |

IN-SEASON

Week 30 In-Season Block C

	Program/activity	Sets/repetitions
MONDAY	**POWER AND QUICKNESS**	
	Puck bash	8 reps at 15 feet
	Circle shuttle	(10:50) 8 reps
	FLEXIBILITY	
	Sequence program	1 × 10-20 sec HRR

TUES	**GAME**

	Program/activity	Sets/repetitions
WEDNESDAY	**AEROBIC**	
	Level 9	
	POWER AND QUICKNESS	
	Skaters—your shot drill	10 reps
	Goalies—lateral-movement drill	8 reps
	FLEXIBILITY	
	Sequence program	1 × 10-20 sec HRR

	Program/activity	Sets/repetitions
THUR	**FLEXIBILITY**	
	Sequence program	1 × 10-20 sec HRR

FRI	**GAME**

SAT	**GAME**

SUN	**DAY OFF**

Week 31 In-Season Block C

	Program/activity	Sets/repetitions	
MONDAY	**AEROBIC**		
	Select level 7, 8, or 9		
	STRENGTH		
	Core program	2 sets, 4-6 reps	
	Unstable workout	1 set, 6-8 reps, all 2-1-2 tempo	
	FLEXIBILITY		
	Sequence program	1 × 10-20 sec HRR	

	Program/activity	Sets/repetitions	
TUESDAY	**POWER AND QUICKNESS**		
	Forwards—quick-corner drill	8 reps	
	Defense—walk-and-shoot drill	8 reps	
	Goalies—telescoping	10 reps	
	FLEXIBILITY		
	Sequence program	1 × 10-20 sec HRR	

WED	**GAME**	

	Program/activity	Sets/repetitions	
THURSDAY	**COMBINATION**		
	Level 2	4 reps	
	POWER AND QUICKNESS		
	Skaters—slot drill	(10:50) 8 reps	
	Goalies—scramble drill	(10:50) 8 reps	
	Everyone—circle shuttle	(10:50) 10 reps	
	FLEXIBILITY		
	Sequence program	1 × 10-20 sec HRR	

FRI	**FLEXIBILITY**	
	Sequence program	1 × 10-20 sec HRR

IN-SEASON

	Program/activity	Sets/repetitions
SAT	GAME	

	Program/activity	Sets/repetitions
SUN	FLEXIBILITY	
	Sequence program	1 × 10-20 sec HRR

Week 32 In-Season Block C

	Program/activity	Sets/repetitions
MON	GAME	

	Program/activity	Sets/repetitions
TUES	DAY OFF	

WEDNESDAY	COMBINATION	
	Level 1	8 reps
	SPEED	
	Line ladder drill	8 reps
	FLEXIBILITY	
	Sequence program	1 × 10-20 sec HRR

THUR	FLEXIBILITY	
	Sequence program	1 × 10-20 sec HRR

FRI	GAME	

SAT	FLEXIBILITY	
	Sequence program	1 × 10-20 sec HRR

SUN	GAME	

Week 33 In-Season Block C

	Program/activity	Sets/repetitions
MON	**FLEXIBILITY**	
	Sequence program	1 × 10-20 sec HRR

TUES	**GAME**	

WED	**GAME**	

THUR	**DAY OFF**	

	Program/activity	Sets/repetitions
FRIDAY	**POWER AND QUICKNESS**	
	Skaters—quick-shot drill	8 reps
	Goalies—wraparound drill	8 reps
	FLEXIBILITY	
	Sequence program	1 × 10-20 sec HRR

SAT	**GAME**	

SUN	**DAY OFF**	

Week 34 In-Season Block C

IN-SEASON

MONDAY

Program/activity	Sets/repetitions
STRENGTH	
Core program	2 sets, 4-6 reps
Unstable workout	1 set, 6-8 reps, all 2-1-2 tempo
POWER AND QUICKNESS	
Incline blast	(10:50) 10 reps, 2 sets
Arm step-ups	(10:50) 10 reps, 2 sets
FLEXIBILITY	
Sequence program	1 × 10-20 sec HRR

TUESDAY

Program/activity	Sets/repetitions
COMBINATION	
Level 4	8 reps
POWER AND QUICKNESS	
Skaters—figure-8 pass drill	8 reps
Quick-release drill	8 reps
Goalies—down-up shot drill	8 reps
FLEXIBILITY	
Sequence program	1 × 10-20 sec HRR

WEDNESDAY

Program/activity	Sets/repetitions
COMBINATION	
Level 1	8 reps
SPEED	
Skaters—on-ice long shift	(45:45) 6 reps
Goalies—five-point shooting	8 reps
FLEXIBILITY	
Sequence program	1 × 10-20 sec HRR

THURSDAY		
AEROBIC		
Select level 7, 8, or 9		
POWER AND QUICKNESS		
Puck bash	10 reps at 15 feet	
Circle shuttle	(10:50) 10 reps	
FLEXIBILITY		
Sequence program	1 × 10-20 sec HRR	

FRI		
FLEXIBILITY		
Sequence program	1 × 10-20 sec HRR	

SAT	
GAME	

SUN	
GAME	

Week 35 In-Season Block C

	Program/activity	Sets/repetitions
MON	DAY OFF	

TUESDAY	**POWER AND QUICKNESS**	
	Forwards—shooting drill	8 reps
	Defense—1-on-1 quick-up drill	8 reps
	Goalies—scramble drill	(10:50) 10 reps
	FLEXIBILITY	
	Sequence program	1 × 10-20 sec HRR

	Program/activity	Sets/repetitions
WED	GAME	

	Program/activity	Sets/repetitions
THUR	FLEXIBILITY	
	Sequence program	1 × 10-20 sec HRR

	Program/activity	Sets/repetitions
FRI	GAME	

	Program/activity	Sets/repetitions
SAT	FLEXIBILITY	
	Sequence program	1 × 10-20 sec HRR

	Program/activity	Sets/repetitions
SUN	GAME	

Week 36 In-Season Block D

	Program/activity	Sets/repetitions
MONDAY	STRENGTH	
	Core program	2 sets, 4-6 reps
	Unstable workout	1 set, 6-8 reps, all 2-1-2 tempo
	COMBINATION	
	Level 1	8 reps
	FLEXIBILITY	
	Sequence program	1 × 10-20 sec HRR

TUESDAY

POWER AND QUICKNESS	
Puck bash	8 reps at 15 feet
Circle shuttle	(10:50) 8 reps
FLEXIBILITY	
Sequence program	1 × 10-20 sec HRR

WED

GAME

THURSDAY

COMBINATION	
Level 3	6 reps
POWER AND QUICKNESS	
Skaters—your shot drill	10 reps
Goalies—scramble drill	(10:50) 10 reps
Everyone—center shuttle	On 45 sec, 10 reps
FLEXIBILITY	
Sequence program	1 × 10-20 sec HRR

FRI

FLEXIBILITY	
Sequence program	1 × 10-20 sec HRR

SAT

GAME

SUN

DAY OFF

IN-SEASON

Week 37 In-Season Block D

	Program/activity	Sets/repetitions
MONDAY	**POWER AND QUICKNESS**	
	Skaters—quick-release drill	8 reps
	Goalies—wraparound drill	8 reps
	FLEXIBILITY	
	Sequence program	1 × 10-20 sec HRR

TUES	**GAME**	

WEDNESDAY	**COMBINATION**	
	Level 1	8 reps
	SPEED	
	Skaters—line ladder drill	8 reps
	Goalies—five-point shooting	8 reps
	FLEXIBILITY	
	Sequence program	1 × 10-20 sec HRR

THUR	**FLEXIBILITY**	
	Sequence program	1 × 10-20 sec HRR

FRI	**GAME**	

SAT	**GAME**	

SUN	**FLEXIBILITY**	
	Sequence program	1 × 10-20 sec HRR

Week 38 In-Season Block D

	Program/activity	Sets/repetitions
MON	GAME	

	Program/activity	Sets/repetitions
TUES	DAY OFF	

	Program/activity	Sets/repetitions
WEDNESDAY	**POWER AND QUICKNESS**	
	Puck bash	8 reps at 20 feet
	Circle shuttle	(10:30) 8 reps
	FLEXIBILITY	
	Sequence program	1 × 10-20 sec HRR

	Program/activity	Sets/repetitions
THUR	GAME	

	Program/activity	Sets/repetitions
FRI	**FLEXIBILITY**	
	Sequence program	1 × 10-20 sec HRR

	Program/activity	Sets/repetitions
SAT	GAME	

	Program/activity	Sets/repetitions
SUN	GAME	

Week 39 In-Season Block D

	Program/activity	Sets/repetitions
MON	**DAY OFF**	

		Program/activity	Sets/repetitions
TUESDAY	**POWER AND QUICKNESS**		
		Skaters—figure-8 pass drill	8 reps
		Quick-shot drill	8 reps
		Goalies—lateral-movement drill	8 reps
	FLEXIBILITY		
		Sequence program	1 × 10-20 sec HRR

	Program/activity	Sets/repetitions
WED	**GAME**	

		Program/activity	Sets/repetitions
THURSDAY	**AEROBIC**		
		Level 9	
	STRENGTH		
		Core program	2 sets, 4-6 reps
		Unstable workout	1 set, 6-8 reps, all 2-1-2 tempo
	FLEXIBILITY		
		Sequence program	1 × 10-20 sec HRR

		Program/activity	Sets/repetitions
FRIDAY	**POWER AND QUICKNESS**		
		Skaters—slot drill	(10:50) 8 reps
		Goalies—down-ups	(10:50) 8 reps
		Everyone—center shuttle	On 1 min, 8 reps
	FLEXIBILITY		
		Sequence program	1 × 10-20 sec HRR

	Program/activity	Sets/repetitions
SAT	**GAME**	

	Program/activity	Sets/repetitions
SUN	**DAY OFF**	

Week 40 In-Season Block D

	Program/activity	Sets/repetitions
MONDAY	**POWER AND QUICKNESS**	
	Forwards—quick-corner drill	8 reps
	Defense—walk-and-shoot drill	8 reps
	Goalies—telescoping	10 reps
	FLEXIBILITY	
	Sequence program	1 × 10-20 sec HRR

TUES	**GAME**	

WED	**COMBINATION**	
	Level 1	6 reps
	FLEXIBILITY	
	Sequence program	1 × 10-20 sec HRR

THUR	**FLEXIBILITY**	
	Sequence program	1 × 10-20 sec HRR

FRI	**GAME**	

SAT	**GAME**	

SUN	**DAY OFF**	

Week 41 In-Season Block D

	Program/activity	Sets/repetitions
MON	GAME	

	Program/activity	Sets/repetitions
TUES	FLEXIBILITY	
	Sequence program	1 × 10-20 sec HRR

	Program/activity	Sets/repetitions
WED	GAME	

	Program/activity	Sets/repetitions
THUR	FLEXIBILITY	
	Sequence program	1 × 10-20 sec HRR

	Program/activity	Sets/repetitions
FRI	GAME	

	Program/activity	Sets/repetitions
SAT	FLEXIBILITY	
	Sequence program	1 × 10-20 sec HRR

	Program/activity	Sets/repetitions
SUN	GAME	

Week 42 In-Season Block E

	Program/activity	Sets/repetitions
MON	FLEXIBILITY	
	Sequence program	1 × 10-20 sec HRR

	Program/activity	Sets/repetitions
TUES	GAME	

WEDNESDAY	COMBINATION	
	Level 4	8 reps
	POWER AND QUICKNESS	
	Puck bash	10 reps at 15 feet
	Circle shuttle	(10:50) 8 reps
	FLEXIBILITY	
	Sequence program	1 × 10-20 sec HRR

THURSDAY	AEROBIC	
	Level 7	
	POWER AND QUICKNESS	
	Skaters—slot drill	(10:50) 8 reps
	Goalies—down-ups	(10:50) 8 reps
	Everyone—center shuttle	On 1 min, 8 reps
	FLEXIBILITY	
	Sequence program	1 × 10-20 sec HRR

FRI	FLEXIBILITY	
	Sequence program	1 × 10-20 sec HRR

SAT	GAME	

SUN	DAY OFF	

Week 43 In-Season Block E

MONDAY

Program/activity	Sets/repetitions
STRENGTH	
Core program	2 sets, 4-6 reps
Unstable workout	1 set, 6-8 reps, all 2-1-2 tempo
POWER AND QUICKNESS	
Incline blast	(10:50) 10 reps
Arm step-ups	(10:50) 10 reps
FLEXIBILITY	
Sequence program	1 × 10-20 sec HRR

TUESDAY

Program/activity	Sets/repetitions
COMBINATION	
Level 1	6 reps
SPEED	
Skaters—line ladder drill	6 reps
Goalies—five-point shooting	8 reps
FLEXIBILITY	
Sequence program	1 × 10-20 sec HRR

WEDNESDAY

Program/activity	Sets/repetitions
AEROBIC	
Level 7	
POWER AND QUICKNESS	
Skaters—figure-8 pass drill	8 reps
Quick-shot drill	8 reps
Goalies—wraparound drill	8 reps
FLEXIBILITY	
Sequence program	1 × 10-20 sec HRR

THUR

Program/activity	Sets/repetitions
FLEXIBILITY	
Sequence program	1 × 10-20 sec HRR

FRI	GAME	
SAT	GAME	
SUN	DAY OFF	

Week 44 In-Season Block E

	Program/activity	Sets/repetitions
MONDAY	**STRENGTH**	
	Core program	2 sets, 4-6 reps
	Unstable workout	1 set, 6-8 reps, all 2-1-2 tempo
	POWER AND QUICKNESS	
	Power push-ups I	12 reps
	Tuck jumps I	12 reps
	Lateral line jumps I	12 reps
	FLEXIBILITY	
	Sequence program	1 × 10-20 sec HRR

	Program/activity	Sets/repetitions
TUESDAY	**COMBINATION**	
	Level 4	6 reps
	POWER AND QUICKNESS	
	Skaters—your shot drill	10 reps
	Goalies—scramble drill	(10:50) 8 reps
	FLEXIBILITY	
	Sequence program	1 × 10-20 sec HRR

	Program/activity	Sets/repetitions
WEDNESDAY	**COMBINATION**	
	Level 1	6 reps
	SPEED	
	On-ice short shift	(30:30) 6 reps
	FLEXIBILITY	
	Sequence program	1 × 10-20 sec HRR

	Program/activity	Sets/repetitions
THURSDAY	**AEROBIC**	
	Level 7	
	POWER AND QUICKNESS	
	Puck bash	10 reps at 15 feet
	Circle shuttle	(10:30) 8 reps
	FLEXIBILITY	
	Sequence program	1 × 10-20 sec HRR

FRI	**FLEXIBILITY**	
	Sequence program	1 × 10-20 sec HRR

SAT	**GAME**	

SUN	**GAME**	

Week 45 In-Season Block E

	Program/activity	Sets/repetitions
MON	**DAY OFF**	

	Program/activity	Sets/repetitions
TUES	**FLEXIBILITY**	
	Sequence program	1 × 10-20 sec HRR

	Program/activity	Sets/repetitions
WED	**GAME**	

	Program/activity	Sets/repetitions
THUR	**FLEXIBILITY**	
	Sequence program	1 × 10-20 sec HRR

	Program/activity	Sets/repetitions
FRI	**GAME**	

	Program/activity	Sets/repetitions
SAT	**FLEXIBILITY**	
	Sequence program	1 × 10-20 sec HRR

	Program/activity	Sets/repetitions
SUN	**GAME**	

IN-SEASON

Week 46 In-Season Block E

IN-SEASON

	Program/activity	Sets/repetitions
MON	DAY OFF	

	Program/activity	Sets/repetitions
TUESDAY	**STRENGTH**	
	Core program	2 sets, 4-6 reps
	Unstable workout	1 set, 6-8 reps, all 2-1-2 tempo
	POWER AND QUICKNESS	
	Skaters—quick-release drill	8 reps
	Goalies—lateral-movement drill	8 reps
	FLEXIBILITY	
	Sequence program	1 × 10-20 sec HRR

WED	**COMBINATION**	
	Level 5	3 reps
	FLEXIBILITY	
	Sequence program	1 × 10-20 sec HRR

THUR	**FLEXIBILITY**	
	Sequence program	1 × 10-20 sec HRR

FRI	GAME	

SAT	GAME	

SUN	DAY OFF	

Week 47 In-Season Block E

	Program/activity	Sets/repetitions
MONDAY	**AEROBIC**	
	Level 7	
	POWER AND QUICKNESS	
	Forwards—quick-corner drill	8 reps
	Defense—walk-and-shoot drill	8 reps
	Goalies—telescoping	10 reps
	FLEXIBILITY	
	Sequence program	1 × 10-20 sec HRR

TUES	**FLEXIBILITY**	
	Sequence program	1 × 10-20 sec HRR

WED	**GAME**	

THUR	**FLEXIBILITY**	
	Sequence program	1 × 10-20 sec HRR

FRI	**GAME**	

SAT	**FLEXIBILITY**	
	Sequence program	1 × 10-20 sec HRR

SUN	**GAME**	

IN-SEASON

Week 48 In-Season Block E

	Program/activity	Sets/repetitions
MON	**DAY OFF**	

	Program/activity	Sets/repetitions
TUES	**FLEXIBILITY**	
	Sequence program	1 × 10-20 sec HRR

	Program/activity	Sets/repetitions
WED	**GAME**	

	Program/activity	Sets/repetitions
THURSDAY	**AEROBIC**	
	Level 7	
	POWER AND QUICKNESS	
	Puck bash	10 reps at 20 feet
	Circle shuttle	(10:30) 10 reps
	FLEXIBILITY	
	Sequence program	1 × 10-20 sec HRR

	Program/activity	Sets/repetitions
FRI	**FLEXIBILITY**	
	Sequence program	1 × 10-20 sec HRR

	Program/activity	Sets/repetitions
SAT	**GAME**	

	Program/activity	Sets/repetitions
SUN	**GAME**	

Chapter

4

Postseason Workouts

"If you have tried to do something and failed, you are vastly better off than if you had tried to do nothing and succeeded."—**Lloyd Jones**

Congratulations on all your hard work. You certainly have the right to feel a sense of accomplishment. Presumably, you learned a few things along the way and are now better prepared to pick up the gauntlet for next season. Before you do, partake in the five Rs—rest, relaxation, rehabilitation, recovery, and reflection. Working through that list is your training job for the postseason, and you should take a month or so to do it.

Note that you don't have to do all those items at once. But you do have to do each of them. They are as important to effective training as building your fitness base in the off-season was. Your mind and body cannot go in high gear every day of the year and keep improving. You need a break to rejuvenate yourself.

Postseason training with the five Rs includes both mind and body components. Training in the other three seasons did too, but the specifics were beyond the scope of this book and in the hands of the sport psychologists. You recognize that it took a coordinated effort of both mind and body to create a successful season. Both, therefore, need to be relieved of pressure and responsibility to become completely refreshed, which is the ultimate goal of postseason training. The mental aspect of postseason training in the *52-Week* program is served by relaxation items. You may refer to them as "mental health breaks."

Consider the five Rs more closely. For rest, relaxation, and recovery, you start with a complete change of pace. Let tired, strained muscles do nothing except maybe soak in hot tubs and enjoy massages. Find a peaceful mental focus, like reading or watching boats go by. After enjoying a few days when you never think about pace, move on to a slightly more energetic activity. Make sure that it uses different muscles than hockey does and uses a different rhythm. Swimming and hiking are excellent change-of-pace activities. Rehabilitation is needed if you've suffered a chronic injury. The postseason is the time to have it tended professionally. Then gradually begin rehabilitation with the aim of getting back to what you would consider normal. Toward the end of the postseason, it is time for reflection. Review your past season. Assess situations that created strain, particularly physical strain, and decide what you can do to change that in the coming season. Then put that behind you. Next, assess what you did well last season, physically and mentally. Decide how to reinforce those strengths so that you can do as well or even better. Set your goals and determine how you will achieve them in the coming season.

The following are your postseason "workouts." Feel free to interchange or add recovery items. If you need rehab, substitute rehab for some recovery items; do the reverse if you don't need rehab.

Now it's time to do next to nothing for a short while and succeed at it.

Postseason Workouts

Purpose
- To become renewed, mentally and physically

Focus
- Rest up from physical fatigue
- Relax all mental tension
- Rehabilitate injuries
- Recover from the strain of the season
- Reflect on achievements and then set new goals

Week 49 Postseason

	Program/activity
MONDAY	**REST**
	Sleep in
	RECOVERY
	Eat well (healthy, balanced meals)
	Drink plenty of fluids, especially water

POSTSEASON

TUESDAY	**RELAXATION**
	Read a magazine or book, or visit the library
	Play an easy video game or watch a movie
	REST
	Take an afternoon nap

WED	**REST**
	Sleep in
	RECOVERY
	Take an easy walk or bike ride

THURSDAY	**REHABILITATION**
	Confirm or call for a doctor's appointment if you have chronic injury, or make arrangements with the team trainer for starting rehab
	RECOVERY
	Play with dogs and/or kids

FRIDAY	**RELAXATION**
	Plan a special weekend doing something you've always wanted to do but haven't had the time
	Take a vacation, if possible
	RECOVERY
	Play a game of horseshoes, bocce, or lawn darts with friends

SAT	**DAY OFF**

SUN	**DAY OFF**

POSTSEASON

Week 50 Postseason

	Program/activity	Sets/repetitions
MONDAY	**REST**	
	Sleep at least 8 hours a night	
	RECOVERY	
	Eat well (healthy, balanced meals)	
	Drink plenty of fluids, especially water	
	RELAXATION	
	Explore a new hobby, or pursue an old one	

	Program/activity	Sets/repetitions
TUESDAY	**REHABILITATION**	
	Have surgery or repair as needed, or meet with the team doctors and trainer for evaluation and/or to begin rehab	
	RECOVERY	
	If medical rehabilitation is unnecessary, go for an easy walk, cycle, or swim	
	RELAXATION	
	Start guitar, drum, or other lessons in something you've always wanted to learn but haven't had time for	

	Program/activity	Sets/repetitions
WED	**RECOVERY**	
	Find a book or video on relaxation techniques, such as tai chi or progressive relaxation, and explore the technique	

	Program/activity	Sets/repetitions
THURSDAY	**RECOVERY**	
	Take an easy walk, cycle, swim, inline skate, or golf	
	RELAXATION	
	Practice the lessons you started Tuesday	

	Program/activity	Sets/repetitions
FRIDAY	**RECOVERY**	
	Plan a weekend with friends and/or family	
	Walk the dog or go to a batting cage or driving range	
	RELAXATION	
	Play some billiards, bowling, darts, or miniature golf	

SAT	DAY OFF

SUN	DAY OFF

Week 51 Postseason

	Program/activity
MONDAY	**REST**
	Sleep at least 8 hours a night
	RECOVERY
	Eat well (healthy, balanced meals)
	Drink plenty of fluids, especially water
	RELAXATION
	Spend time on your hobby

TUESDAY	**REFLECTION**
	Start a hockey journal, with the first entry being a general, candid evaluation of your game
	RECOVERY
	Play some recreational baseball, soccer, or golf, or check out a new park or hiking/biking trail
	Practice the relaxation technique of your choice

WEDNESDAY	**REHABILITATION**
	Do rehabilitation of injury or surgery (may be a daily activity)
	REFLECTION
	Make a list of all the hockey things you did well last season
	RELAXATION
	Have a music night—listening or playing

	Program/activity
THUR	**RECOVERY**
	Explore an activity you have not done, such as canoeing, kayaking, hiking, or rock climbing

FRIDAY	**REFLECTION**
	Add to Wednesday's list; circle your strengths
	RECOVERY
	Make plans for an active weekend with friends and/or family, such as camping, fishing, hiking, or a canoe trip

SAT	**DAY OFF**

SUN	**DAY OFF**

Week 52 Postseason

	Program/activity
MONDAY	**REST**
	Sleep at least 8 hours a night
	RECOVERY
	Eat well (healthy, balanced meals)
	Drink plenty of fluids, especially water
	REHABILITATION
	Do your rehab program
	RELAXATION
	Spend time on your hobby

TUESDAY	**RECOVERY**	
	Do an enjoyable recreational activity	
	REFLECTION	
	Make a list of things you want to improve or change in the next hockey season	

WED	**RECOVERY**	
	Practice the relaxation technique of your choice	
	REFLECTION	
	Add a second column to Tuesday's list that declares what you will do to change each item listed	

THUR	**RECOVERY**	
	Do an enjoyable recreational activity	
	REFLECTION	
	Write down your personal goals for next season; set progressive, high, achievable targets	

FRIDAY	**RELAXATION AND RECOVERY**	
	Plan an enjoyable, relaxing weekend	
	REFLECTION	
	Add a second column to Thursday's list, filling in how you plan to accomplish each goal; be sure to make maximum use of your strengths and indicate how you will improve or compensate for your weaknesses	

SAT	**DAY OFF**

SUN	**DAY OFF**

POSTSEASON

PART II

Exercises and Drills

Part II explains the precise techniques used in *52-Week Hockey Training* to train all the elements of fitness a hockey player needs for high performance. Each exercise and drill used in the program is explained and most are illustrated. All terms, such as tempo, resistance, and pace, are explained. Each fitness element is presented by chapter, beginning with chapter 5 for flexibility, chapter 6 for muscle strength and endurance, chapter 7 for aerobic endurance, chapter 8 for speed, and chapter 9 for power and quickness. Each chapter concludes with a list of alternative exercises. These can be substituted for some of those in the *52-Week* program if players want more variety or if they have access to different equipment.

Chapter 5

Flexibility

"What stops being better stops being good."—**Oliver Cromwell**

Athletes have used a variety of stretching techniques over the years. Some techniques improve flexibility, some don't, and some are counterproductive. The *52-Week Hockey Training* program recommends that players use the stretch-relaxation technique for optimum improvement of flexibility.

The technique is very specific: stretch to a point of mild tension, hold that position while you relax and drain out the tension, stretch slightly farther to a new point of tension, hold again and relax what has tightened, and then repeat to a third point of tension.

Each workout specifies the time to take for the three stretch-hold-relax-repeat phases (identified as HRR in the workouts). The duration of HRR changes through the seasons as players' flexibility improves.

Note that dynamic stretching (bouncing, swinging) is useful at the conclusion of a warm-up to ensure that you are loosened up, but it does not improve flexibility. For improvement and good maintenance, use the stretch-relaxation technique, ideally at the end of every practice. Performing the technique at that time provides the added benefit of reducing muscle soreness that often follows hard practices or training sessions.

The *52-Week Hockey Training* program places all stretches into four sequences for ease and thoroughness of training. Do all four sequences each workout, performing them as follows.

Sequence Flexibility Program Exercises

Squat Sequence

- Start in squat position. Press your heels toward the floor (photo a). HRR.
- Extend your legs slowly to standing toe-touch position with your knees straight but not locked. Press your stomach to your thighs (photo b). HRR.
- Slowly uncurl to erect position as if straightening from hips to head, one vertebra at a time (photo c). Relax throughout.

a

b

c

Lateral and Shoulder Sequence

- Start in a lateral lunge position with your feet parallel and the foot of the extended leg flat on the floor. Rest your torso on the bent leg (photo a). HRR.
- Slowly extend the bent knee as you hug your torso to your thigh (photo b). HRR.
- Release the leg and move your torso to the center. Press your chest toward the floor. HRR.
- Repeat the lateral lunge to the other side. HRR, then extend, HRR, and center HRR.
- Slowly uncurl to an upright position as you did in the squat sequence.

a

b

(continued)

c

d

e

- Reduce but retain a straddle stance. Lean your torso to the right. Slide your left arm overhead but keep it relaxed. HRR. Extend your left arm and reach to the right (photo c). HRR. Do not twist.
- Repeat torso stretch to the left side with HRRs.
- From an erect position further reduce the straddle stance. Twist your torso from the hips to the right as far as possible (photo d). HRR. Repeat to the left. HRR.
- Fix your right hand against a wall in front at shoulder height and arm's length. Turn your body as far away from the wall as possible (photo e). HRR. Repeat with the left hand. HRR.

- Clasp your left elbow with your right hand as though in a choke hold. Press with the right (photo f). HRR. Lift your left elbow overhead (with your hand hanging down the back of your neck) and press at the elbow with the right hand (photo g). HRR. Repeat for the right shoulder with HRRs.
- Clasp your hands and press overhead as high as possible (photo h). HRR. Clasp your hands behind your back, with arms straight, and press up as high as possible without bending forward. HRR.

f

g

h

Seven-Point Sequence

- Start in the front straddle position with toes pointing forward. Press the back heel to the floor, keep your leg straight, and bend the front knee (photo a). HRR. Press the back knee toward the floor, keeping the back heel on the floor (photo b). HRR. Reverse leg position and repeat with HRRs.
- Drop to one knee and extend the other leg straight back so that the top of your foot is on the floor. Press your torso back (photo c). HRR. Repeat for the other leg. HRR.
- Sit with the left foot on the outside of the right knee while the right leg is extended. Clasp your bent knee and press toward the opposite shoulder (photo d). HRR. Repeat for the other leg. HRR.
- Sit with the soles of your feet together, your hands clasping your ankles, and your elbows on your knees. Press your knees toward the floor (photo e). HRR.
- Roll onto your side. Bend the upper knee so that you can clasp that ankle with your upper hand. Keeping thigh parallel to floor, press your heel toward your buttocks (photo f). HRR. Repeat for the other leg. HRR.
- Lie on your stomach. Place your hands under your shoulders and extend your arms, leaving your hips on the floor (photo g). HRR.
- Roll onto your back. Press your heels toward the ceiling and the small of your back to the floor. HRR. Tuck and hug your knees to your chest (photo h). HRR.

a

b

c

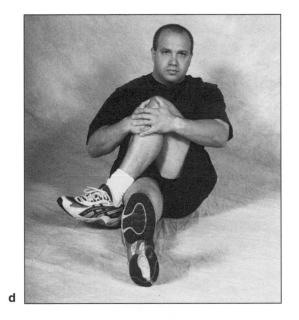

d

e

f

(continued)

g

h

Wrist and Ankle Sequence

- From your previous back-lying position, flex and then extend your ankles. HRR at each position.
- Then pronate, supinate, and slowly rotate each ankle. Repeat for your wrists.

▐F▌lexibility Exercise Substitutes

Long-Sit Stretches (for Calves and Hamstrings)

Sit with your legs straight in front but with knees not locked. Draw your toes toward your knees. HRR. Press your stomach to your thighs. Let your chest and then your head drop to your legs. HRR.

Straddle-Sit Stretches (for Hamstrings, Groin, and Torso)

Sit with your legs extended in straddle position but with knees not locked. Press your stomach to one thigh. Let your chest and then your head drop. HRR. Repeat to the other thigh. HRR. Repeat to center. HRR. Sit erect and then lean to place your elbow on the floor beside your hip. Slowly draw the opposite arm overhead and let it hang. HRR. Repeat to the other side. HRR.

Hurdler's Stretches (for Hamstrings and Quadriceps)

Sit with one leg extended in front and the other leg bent so that the inside of the leg is flat on the floor. Press your stomach to the extended thigh and then let your chest and head drop toward the leg. HRR. Hold the leg position and carefully lower your back to the floor. Press the bent knee toward the floor. HRR. Note that this is not an exercise for those with bad knees.

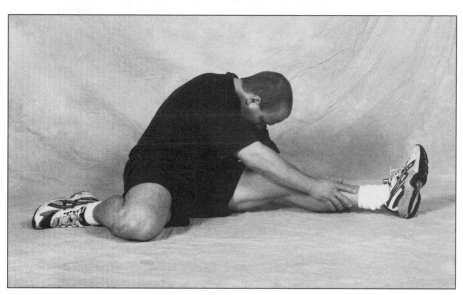

Reverse Hurdler's Stretches (for Hamstrings and Groin)

Sit with one leg extended in front and the foot of the other leg against the thigh of the extended leg. Press your stomach, then your chest, and then your head toward the extended leg while pressing the bent knee toward the floor. HRR. Repeat the press to the center. HRR. Repeat both presses and HRRs with leg positions reversed.

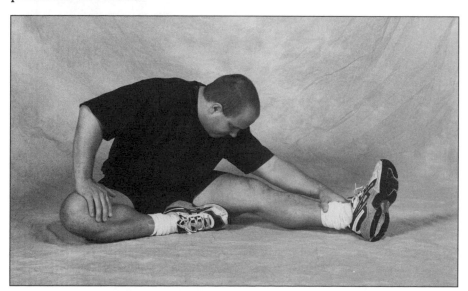

Quad Stretches

The side-lying stretch described in the sequence program can be performed from a standing or kneeling position.

Calf Stretches

Stand with toes only on a raised platform. Lower your heels below your toes. HRR. The single-leg stretch done in sequence can also be performed using a wall or the floor for support. Use the same knee bends and HRRs.

Hip Stretches (for Buttock and Hip Muscles)

Lie on your back with one leg extended. Place the other thigh across the extended hip and let the knee bend. Press that knee toward the floor. HRR. You can modify this exercise by placing the extended leg over the bent knee and using that semiextended leg to press the knee toward the floor. HRR.

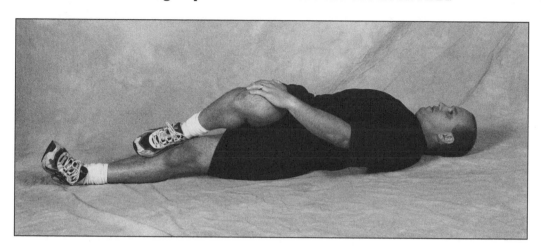

Partner- and Implement-Assisted Stretches

You can perform other kinds of stretches with a partner or by using a towel, rope, or ball. Some of these exercises can help improve flexibility, and you can substitute them for some of the sequence exercises. Consult a book about flexibility exercises. If you wish to use these exercises, be sure to understand which muscle groups they stretch.

Chapter

6

Muscle Strength and Endurance

"Success comes when you know you have the strength to handle any failure."—**G.K. Reynolds**

You can develop muscle strength and endurance by using various kinds of equipment. But whether you use dumbbells or computerized equipment, the principles for improvement stay the same.

Muscle Strength

Resistance and tempo are the keys to improving muscle strength. The resistance necessary for strength gain is 60 to 100 percent of maximum. For practical and safety reasons, most strength programs target 70 to 80 percent of the maximum weight you could lift and still complete the exercise. So you could use a spotter and experiment with heavy weights to find out what your one-repetition max is for each exercise. A 70 or 80 percent target for each exercise would be your starting resistance.

Alternatively, you can start the program using what you would consider to be a medium weight for you. All exercises in the *52-Week* program use three sets with a maximum number of repetitions per set. If on day one you complete the maximum reps in each set comfortably using your medium weight, increase your weight (resistance) each day until you cannot complete the maximum reps in all three sets. For example, with a target maximum of 10 reps, perhaps you can only do 10, 8, and 6 reps in three sets at your medium weight. You would then train each day using that weight until you are able to do three sets of 10 reps each. Progress comes by increasing the weight by two to five pounds (one to two kilograms) each time you work up to being able to complete the three sets of 10 reps (or the maximum number prescribed).

The other important factor in effective strength training is tempo—the speed at which an exercise is performed. If you do an exercise too quickly, you are probably taking advantage of momentum through part of the exercise. Your muscle is not doing the work; therefore, it is not being trained through parts of the exercise. Your muscle is made up of thousands of muscle fibers. You must train all of them if you want strength through the complete range of movement. The other concern about tempo is that you must perform virtually all movements in hockey at high speed. If you train muscles too slowly, they are effective only for slow pace. The *52-Week* strength-training program specifies the tempo and varies it so that your muscles are trained through their full range and become able to use their strength at high speed. This sort of training contributes to what you recognize as power in a movement.

Tempo is indicated in the workouts by three numbers, such as 4-2-4. That designation means that the eccentric or initial movement in the exercise is to take four seconds. You hold the end position for two seconds and then take four seconds to return to your starting position. This is the concentric part of the exercise. For example, in the bench press, you would count four seconds as you lower the bar to your chest, two seconds as you hold the bar at your chest, and then four seconds as you press the bar back up to the starting position. Tempos are slower in the early training to establish a safe strength base. Later, tempos increase to add power and specificity.

The *52-Week* strength-training program includes both a core strength program that uses traditional strength exercises and an unstable workout that uses the Swiss ball. Unstable workouts help make the strength you gain more applicable to hockey skills.

The unstable workouts provide advanced strength training. If you do not feel you can perform the unstable exercises correctly and safely, stay with the core program until you develop a greater strength base. You may want to phase in some unstable exercises and gradually build up to a complete unstable workout.

Safety is an important factor in any strength-training program. The following tips will help you maximize progress and avoid injury.

1. Use the correct technique to perform each exercise. All the exercises used in the program are explained and illustrated. Confirm your technique.
2. Breathe properly while exercising. Holding your breath can cause dizziness or fainting. Breathe out during the work phases (eccentric and concentric) and breathe in during the hold phase.
3. Work with a partner so that you can spot for each other.
4. Check that all equipment is safe before you exercise.
5. Do not use weight belts or straps while performing exercises. Use your muscles.

Core Strength-Training Program Exercises

Bench Press

Lie with your back flat on the bench and feet flat on the floor. Grip the bar with your palms up and hands shoulder-width apart. Start with your arms fully extended and lower the bar straight down until it touches your chest. Hold. Then return the bar to the start position.

Incline Bench Press

Have your back flat against the incline bench and feet flat on the floor. Grip the bar with your palms up and hands shoulder-width apart. Start with the arms extended and lower the bar straight down until it touches your chest. Hold. Then return to the start position. You can also do the exercise using dumbbells.

Military Press

Sit at the end of a bench with your feet flat on the floor and thighs parallel to the floor. Start with the bar at chest level. Use a palms-up grip with hands shoulder-width apart. Lift the weight straight over your head until your arms are fully extended. Hold. Return to the start position.

Pull-Downs

Sit or kneel with your feet secure and use a palms-down grip. Pull the bar down to your chest. Hold. Return to the start position. A variation is to pull the bar down behind your head to the shoulders. Hold and return to the start position.

Biceps Curls

Use dumbbells and a palms-up grip. Your shoulders and buttocks should be against a wall with your feet out from the wall. Start with the dumbbells at your side. Using your arms alternately, raise a dumbbell until it touches your chest. Hold. Return to the start position.

Triceps Curls

Sit or stand and start with a dumbbell directly above your head. Lower the dumbbell until it touches your back. Hold. Return to the start position.

Wrist Curls

Sit with your thighs parallel to the floor. Grip the dumbbell with palms up. Have your forearm flat on your thigh with the wrist in front of the knee to allow free wrist movement. Roll the dumbbell down toward the floor as far as possible (to fingertips) while keeping the elbow and forearm in contact with your thigh. Hold. Roll the dumbbell up as high as possible.

Sit-Ups

Place a weight plate against your chest with your arms crossed against your chest to secure the weight. Bend your knees and place your feet flat on the floor. Curl up to touch your knees. Hold. Return to the lying position.

Back Extension

Place a weight plate against your chest with your arms crossed against your chest to secure the weight. Lie on a bench from your hips down with your feet secured. Lower your torso toward the floor. Raise your torso as high as possible. Hold. Return to the start position.

Lateral Raises

Place a weight plate against your chest with your arms crossed against your chest to secure the weight. Lie on your side with your hips perpendicular to the floor and your feet secured. Curl your torso up as far as possible toward your hip. Hold. Return to the start position. Do not let your hips roll forward or back. Use only the side muscles to lift and lower your torso.

Squats

With a barbell resting across your shoulders behind your neck, use your arms to stabilize the bar. Keep your head up and chest out. Your feet should be flat on the floor and shoulder-width apart. With a slight forward bend at the waist, bend your legs until you reach a 90-degree angle at the knees. Hold. Return to the start position.

Leg Flexion

Lie on your stomach on a bench with your feet against resistance and your hands holding on to stabilize the upper body. Pull your heels up toward your buttocks. Hold. Return to the start position.

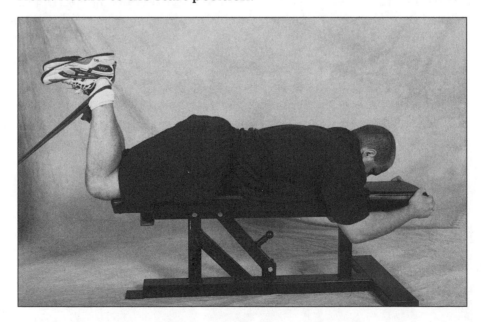

Leg Extension

Sit on a bench with your feet against resistance and your hands holding on to stabilize the upper body. Push upward until your legs are straight. Hold. Return to the start position.

Heel Raises

With a barbell resting on your shoulders and stabilized using your hands, have your toes elevated (e.g., on a box) and your heels touching the floor. Raise your heels as far as possible off the floor. Hold. Return to the start position.

Lateral Leg Pulls

Inside—With resistance attached to your ankle, your leg straight, and your foot slightly elevated from the floor, pull your foot from a position outside the normal standing stance across and in front of the other foot, extending as far as possible. Hold. Return to the start position. Outside—Use the same motion but apply the resistance in the opposite direction as you pull your foot away from your body.

Unstable Workout Exercises

Dumbbell Press

Sit on a ball holding dumbbells at your shoulders and your elbows at your side. Push one dumbbell straight over your head. Hold. Return to the start position. Alternate dumbbells.

Dumbbell Pullovers

Place your head and shoulders on a ball. Keep your body straight and your feet flat on the floor with a 90-degree bend at the knees, bridging on the ball. Hold a dumbbell with both hands straight overhead. Lower the dumbbell behind your head until it touches the ball. Hold. Return to the start position.

Chin-Ups

Place your feet on a ball and keep your body straight along the floor with your chest under a fixed bar. Use a palms-down grip with your hands shoulder-width apart. Pull your body up to the bar. Hold. Return to the start position.

Biceps Curls

Place your chest and elbows on a ball and hold your legs straight with toes on the floor. Start by holding dumbbells with arms extended. Alternately curl the dumbbells up to your body. Hold. Return to the start position.

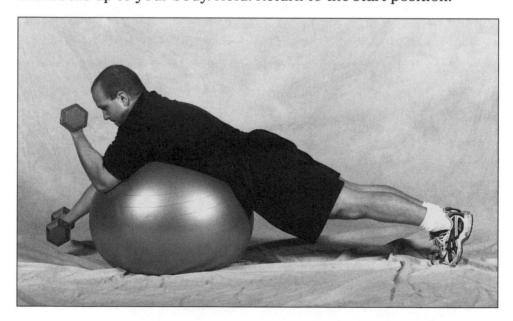

Triceps Curls

Sit on a ball with your feet flat on the floor. Hold a dumbbell overhead. Drop the weight behind your head until it touches your shoulders. Hold. Return to the start position.

Wrist Curls

Sit on a ball with your feet flat on the floor and thighs parallel to the floor. Hold a dumbbell with a palms-up grip. Keep your forearms on your thigh with your wrist in front of the knee. Roll the dumbbell down as low as possible. Hold. Roll your wrist up as far as possible.

Bridging

Place your shoulders and head on a ball. Make trunk parallel to floor. Hold.

Bridging With Rotation

Using the bridging position, hold a weight plate and rotate first to the left side of the body and then to the right.

Supine With Feet on Ball

Lie with your back on the floor, knees bent, and your feet on a ball. Your hands are on your hips. Straighten your legs so that your body is straight with your hips off the floor. Hold.

Back Extension

Lie with your stomach on a ball and your feet on the floor. Your hands touch your head. Raise your upper body as high as possible. Hold. Lower your upper body as low as possible. Repeat.

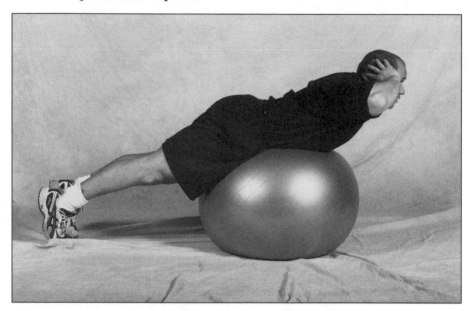

One-Leg Squats

Place your left foot on a ball and your right leg in front of the ball. Hold a weight plate over your head with your arms straight. Perform a squat technique until you reach a 90-degree bend in your right leg. Hold. Return to the straight-leg stance.

One-Leg Curls

With your back and shoulders on the floor and your hands on your hips, place both feet on a ball. Raise one leg and roll the ball toward your hips, doing a curl motion with the leg that is on the ball until your foot is flat on the ball. Hold. Return to the start position. Repeat with the other leg. You can also do the exercise using both legs.

Hip Flexion

Place your body parallel to the floor in push-up position with your feet on the ball. Raise your right leg slightly off the ball. Roll the ball forward using your left leg until your foot touches your buttocks. Hold. Return to the start position.

Hip Extension

Place a ball on a bench. Lie with your stomach on the ball, your legs bent, and your thighs against the ball. Hold on to the bench with your hands. Raise your thighs as far from the ball as possible. Hold. Return to the start position.

Wall Squats

Place a ball between your right shoulder and a wall. Hold your right foot off the floor. Your left foot is outside your body to create a lean toward the wall. Roll the ball up and down the wall by straightening and bending your left leg.

Alternative Strength-Training Exercises

░ General

Dumbbells

Exercises normally performed with a barbell can be done with dumbbells instead. Use the same technique and tempo. You can perform the exercises in two ways:

1. Use both dumbbells at the same time (just as you would use a bar).
2. Alternate, using one dumbbell at a time.

Calisthenics

If equipment is not available, you can use your body weight for resistance. The following are examples of body-weight exercises that you can substitute for the strength exercises of the program (in parentheses).

Push-ups (bench press)—Have resistance at your shoulders.

Raised push-ups (incline bench press)—Have your feet elevated on a bench while you perform push-ups.

Chin-ups (military press and pull-downs)—Have your palms up when gripping the bar.

Chin-ups (biceps)—Have your palms down when gripping the bar.

Bench dips (triceps)—Have your feet elevated on one bench and grip the edge of another bench. Start with your body parallel to the floor. Lower your body toward the floor as low as possible. Pause. Return to the start position.

Stick roll (wrists)—Use a stick with a weight attached by a cord three feet (one meter) long. Hold the stick in both hands with your palms down and arms straight in front (parallel to the floor). Roll your wrists until the weight makes contact with the stick. Pause. Return the weight to the start position by rolling your wrists in the reverse direction. You can do the exercise with palms up as well. See photo above.

Lower-Body Exercises

Single-Leg Squats

Hold a weight plate overhead and slightly back and then raise one foot behind your body toward your buttocks. Perform a squat with the other leg by lowering your upper body toward the floor until you reach a 90-degree bend in the knee. Pause. Return to the start position. Complete all reps with one leg and then switch to the other leg.

Single-Leg Flexion

Perform the regular leg flexion exercise using only one leg. Use less resistance than you did with the double-leg flexion. Use proper technique.

Single-Leg Extension

Perform the regular leg extension except use one leg at a time.

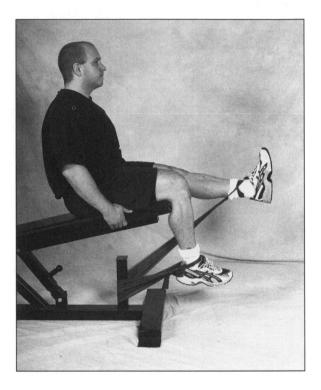

Lunges

Simulate an exaggerated skating stride as you step laterally right into a deep knee bend. Then push off left for another stride. You can also do lunges to make forward progress. Hold a weight at your chest or overhead.

Deadlift

With a barbell on the floor, position your feet shoulder-width apart and under the bar. Bend down to grasp the bar with a reverse grip (one palm forward, the other backward), keep the upper body erect, and bend your knees beyond 90 degrees. Lift with the legs, not the back.

Abdominal Exercise

Hanging Tucks

Using a dip or chin-up bar, start with your body vertical. Draw your knees to your chest. Hold. Lower to vertical. A more difficult level of this exercise is to lift straight legs to the horizontal position. Hold, then lower.

Shoulder Exercises

Side Dumbbell Raises

Start by holding dumbbells by your side. Raise the dumbbells straight up to the side as high above shoulder height as possible. Hold. Return to the start position.

Front Dumbbell Raises

Start by holding dumbbells by your side. Raise the dumbbells straight in front of your body as high above shoulder height as possible. Hold. Return to the start position.

Behind-the-Neck Military Press

Using the technique you used for the military press, lower the bar behind your head until the bar touches your neck. Hold. Return to the start position.

Shrugs

Holding dumbbells by your side, rotate your shoulders in a circular motion, making the largest circle possible. Alternate clockwise and counterclockwise circles with each set.

Upright Rowing

Standing with your feet shoulder-width apart and body erect, hold a barbell in front of your body with a palms-down grip and your arms extended toward the floor. Using a closed grip (hands close together) raise the bar to your chin. Hold. Return to the start position.

Bent-Over Rowing

Stand with your feet shoulder-width apart and your upper body parallel with the floor. Start with your arms straight and a barbell close to the floor. Pull the bar to your chest. Hold. Return to the start position.

Back Exercises

Lateral Pulls

Seated, grip handle in front of your body. Keep your upper body erect and pull the handle toward your body until it makes contact. Hold. Return to the start position.

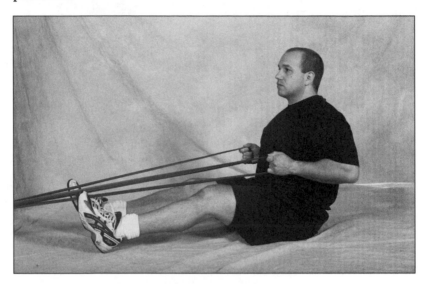

One-Arm Dumbbell Rowing

Start with your right knee and right hand on a bench, your left foot on the floor, a dumbbell in your left hand, and your upper body parallel to the floor. Raise the weight to your chest. Hold. Return to the start position.

Chest Exercises

Close-Grip Bench

Use basic bench press technique. Change position from shoulder-width apart to close together.

Flat Dumbbell Press

Use basic bench press technique. Replace the barbell with a dumbbell in each hand. Push dumbbells at the same time or alternately.

Incline Dumbbell Press

With a bench at 45 degrees, use basic incline press technique, replacing the barbell with dumbbells. Push dumbbells at the same time or alternately.

Flat Dumbbell Flys

With your arms straight overhead, a dumbbell in each hand, and lying face up flat on the bench, lower the weights down and to the side. Hold. Return to the start position.

Incline Dumbbell Flys

Use the technique for the flat dumbbell fly with the bench at 45 degrees.

Arm Exercises

Curl Bar

Do the basic biceps curl using a curl bar instead of a regular barbell.

Triceps Pull-Downs

Grip the bar with a closed grip. Start at shoulder height and push the bar straight down toward the floor until your arms are straight. Hold. Return to the start position.

Dips on Apparatus

Use a dip apparatus. Start with your arms straight, body elevated, and legs bent. Lower your body until the elbow angle is at least 90 degrees. Hold. Return to the start position.

Reverse Wrist Curls

Use the wrist curl technique with a palms-down grip.

Muscle Endurance

Muscle endurance has to do with repeatability, so you must train it in a different way than you train muscle strength. The key to improving muscle endurance is performing repetitions. Keep resistance low to moderate (around 50 percent of maximum) so that you can perform a large number of repetitions. Body weight is often appropriate resistance for this type of training. If an exercise like sit-ups becomes too easy using body weight, add a light free weight.

The *52-Week* muscle endurance program emphasizes upper-body and torso work. The legs receive considerable muscle endurance training through the aerobic program, although the lateral muscles are not usually included. Additional muscle endurance training for the legs is therefore not necessary unless you are swimming or kayaking for aerobic work. If you have access to the equipment, the lateral-slide exercise (using the slider board) is included for working lateral leg muscles. Finally, the core exercises include burpees for some whole-body muscle endurance work.

As in strength training, exercise tempo is important in muscle endurance training, primarily to minimize the tendency to use momentum rather than muscle power. Workouts specify the tempo as being 1/x number of seconds. For example, the workout might specify "20 reps at 1/6 sec," which means that you would execute one complete cycle of the exercise each six seconds. Each half of the exercise should take half the time (three seconds). A metronome is a useful guide for this pacing, but the count "one-one thousand, two-one thousand . . ." can be close enough. Check yourself against a stopwatch.

Periodically, workouts specify that an exercise be performed to exhaustion. Exhaustion is technically when you can no longer maintain the specified tempo. For example, you may be required to do push-ups at one per second. When you fall off that rhythm, you are finished.

By their very nature, burpees cannot be done slowly. From the outset, set a brisk tempo using full extension and explosion for each phase of the exercise. Time that brisk tempo and use that as your exhaustion pace when required.

Core Muscle Endurance Exercises

Twist Sit-Ups

Lie on the floor with your knees bent, your feet flat on the floor, and your fingers touching at the back of your head. Without exerting any pressure on your head, curl up your right elbow to touch your left knee and return to the start position (shoulders touch the floor). Then curl up your left shoulder so that your left elbow touches your right knee and return to the start position. Each touch is one cycle. Be sure to start the twist from the floor, not after you sit up.

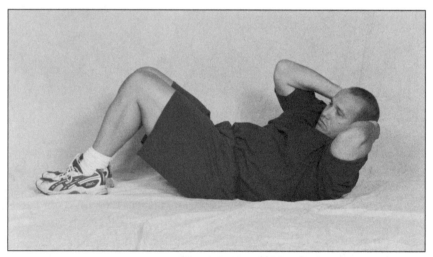

Knee Tucks

Start in a flat, back-lying position, holding your feet just off the floor (one inch or two centimeters). Draw your heels parallel to the floor toward your buttocks as you press the small of your back into the floor. Return to the start position.

Trunk Lifts

Lie face down on a bench from hips down with your feet secured. Let your torso bend toward the floor. Your hands are on your head. Lift your torso until it is parallel to the floor, then lower to the start position.

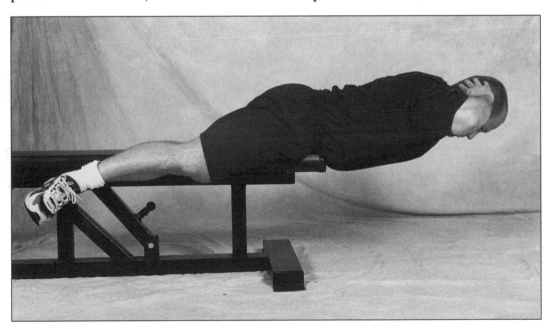

Leg Lifts

Lie face down on a bench from hips up using your arms to secure your torso. Keep your legs straight with your toes touching the floor. Lift your legs until they are parallel to the floor, then lower to the start position. Do not swing your legs up.

Push-Ups

Start face down with your toes on the floor and your hands under your shoulders. Extend your arms, keeping your body straight until your elbows straighten. Then lower to touch your chest and stomach simultaneously to the floor. Keep weight on your hands and toes only.

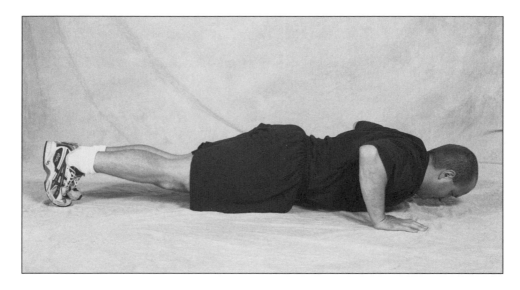

Dips on Bench

Sit on the edge of a bench with your legs straight out so that your heels rest on a second bench (or chair). Grip the edge of the bench beside your hips. Slide your hips off the bench and lower toward the floor as far as possible. Then press up until your elbows are straight.

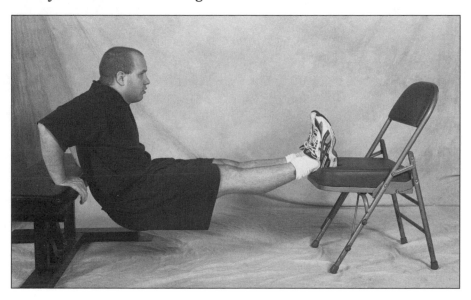

Lateral Curls

Lie on your side on a bench or the floor with your feet secured, hips perpendicular to the floor, and hands on your head. Curl up as though trying to touch your upper elbow to your hip. Then lower until your elbow (for bench) or shoulder (for floor) touches the floor. Repeat the exercise for the other side. Do not curl forward.

Burpees

From a standing position, drop to crouch position, extend to push-up position, return to crouch position, and explode to maximal vertical jump.

a

b

c

Slider Board

Mimic full skating stride to maximum possible.

Alternative Muscle Endurance Exercises

Tuck Sits or V-Sits (for Abdominals)

Start in back-lying position with your legs straight and arms overhead. Simultaneously curl up your torso as you draw your knees to your chest (tuck) or raise your legs straight up (V) as far as possible so that your buttocks alone support the position. Then return to the start position.

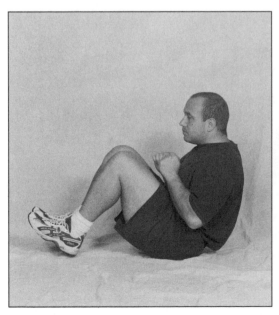

Back Flys

Lie face down with hips on a Swiss ball or narrow, padded bench. Your feet and head are touching the floor, and your hands are on your head. Lift your legs and torso simultaneously until they are parallel to the floor. Hold and then lower to the start position.

Elevated Push-Ups

Use the normal, arm-extended push-up position but place your feet on a Swiss ball, step bench, or box. Lower your chest to touch the floor. Hold. Push up to the start position.

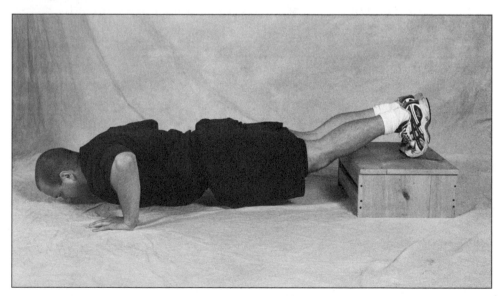

Pull-Ups

Lie on your back facing a horizontal bar that you can just reach above your shoulders. Keep your body straight and your feet in contact with the floor as you pull up as close to the bar as possible. Hold. Lower to touch your shoulders to the floor. The exercise can also be done as incline pull-ups (pictured) using a higher bar.

Hanging Twist Tucks

Hang vertically from a dip or chin-up bar. Draw your right knee up toward your left armpit. Hold. Lower. Repeat with the left knee to the right armpit. The exercise can also be done lifting both legs simultaneously (pictured).

Spin Jumps

Start by standing with your feet close together. Jump on the spot one-quarter turn to the right, back to the start, one-half turn to the right, back to the start, one-quarter turn to the left, back to the start, one-half turn to the left, and back to the start for one repeat.

Chapter 7

Aerobic Endurance

"A professional is someone who can do his best work when he doesn't feel like it."—**Alistair Cooke**

Aerobic training requires the involvement of your whole body because you are trying to challenge the entire network of your heart, lungs, blood supply, and muscles to greater levels of efficiency. For that reason you should use activities like running, cycling, cross-country skiing, in-line skating, rowing machines, or even water running for training. If possible, use a variety of these activities to challenge more muscles.

Regardless of what activities you choose, the key to aerobic improvement is pace. If you don't push hard enough you will not improve; if you push too hard you will compromise your progress.

What pace is just right? Athletes are often told to monitor their heart rate during training for an indication of pace. You start aerobic training at a pace of 170 minus your age for a target heart rate around 150 beats per minute (170 – 20 = 150) and work toward training at 180 beats per minute (200 – 20 = 180).

A pace system developed by Swedish scientist G.A. Borg is more desirable for *52-Week Hockey Training* because of the variety of pace work that is necessary to prepare for the game. Borg's system, the rate of perceived exertion scale, is based on the athlete's honest response to the question "How does the exercise feel?" The scale ranges from "No exertion at all" to "Maximal exertion," as seen in figure 7.1 on the next page.

6	No exertion at all
7	
8	Extremely light
9	Very light
10	
11	Light
12	
13	Somewhat hard
14	
15	Hard (heavy)
16	
17	Very hard
18	
19	Extremely hard
20	Maximal exertion

Borg RPE scale
© Gunnar Borg, 1970, 1985, 1994, 1998

Figure 7.1   Rate of perceived exertion scale.

Reprinted, by permission, from Gunnar Borg, 1998, *Borg's Perceived Exertion and Pain Scales,* (Champaign, IL: Human Kinetics), 47.

The *52-Week* nine-level aerobic progression program asks you to train at paces that are strong and easy. Using Borg's scale, whether you are running, cycling, or cross-country skiing, the strong portion of your training should make you respond to the question "How does the exercise feel?" with an answer such as, "I feel I'm pushing pretty hard" (or "hard" or "quite hard"). That would be more than "somewhat hard," but not quite "very hard," using Borg's terms. In other words, strong ranges from 14 on Borg's scale in the early stages of your training to 16 as you get in shape. Easy, on the other hand, should feel almost light—11.5 to 12 on Borg's scale.

It is also important to know your moderate pace. That approximates a 13 or "somewhat hard" answer on the scale. Knowing your moderate pace helps you more accurately define your strong and easy paces for more effective aerobic training. The training paces for speed and power and quickness (explained in subsequent chapters) also use Borg's scale as a guide. An 18 to 19 (extremely hard) answer is necessary for training speed, and 20 (maximal exertion) is necessary for training power and quickness. These paces are called *all out* for speed and *explosive* for power and quickness in the *52-Week* program. You should play with all of these paces a few times at the beginning of training to feel out the differences between them.

Getting back to aerobics, training at an actual strong pace, as opposed to too hard or more moderate, will make a tremendous difference in your game pace.

In the progressive aerobic program, you start at level 1 in the off-season and go level by level through the progression, no matter what shape you are in at the beginning. If you start in decent shape, you may spend only one day at level 1 and at each of levels 2, 3, and 4. But you may need three sessions of level 5 before moving on. Move to the next higher level when the strong phase of the current level really does feel strong. If you are lumbering through the final minutes of the strong phase, you are not ready for the next level. The aerobic target for high-performance hockey players is level 9 by the end of the off-season. However, levels 7 to 9 will give you a good base for preseason training and keep you in good shape, with proper maintenance, throughout the season. So level 7 is the minimum standard if you suffer a setback, such as an injury, that inhibits your progress.

When building aerobic endurance, you need to find just the right pace so that you challenge yourself but don't overdo it.

Note that the rate movement through the nine-level progression established in the workouts may be too fast or too slow for your condition, so adjust accordingly. If during the season you are inactive for a couple of weeks or longer because of injury, start back at level 1 when you resume training and progress level by level just as you did initially. That approach is the quickest, safest, and most effective way to reestablish your aerobic base. If you fail to reestablish your base, all your hockey skills, power, and training will be negatively affected.

Aerobic exercise notes

- **Running.** Wear high-quality shoes that fit well. Take deep, relaxed breaths. Check that your foot placement is straight forward, not turned out. Hockey players frequently toe out, which places unwanted stress on knee ligaments.
- **Cycling.** A stationary bike can be more effective than a free-wheel bike because resistance and coasting are easier to control. If you do cycle outside,

chart your course to minimize downhill slopes and steep climbs. With either type of bike, check that your seat placement is directly over the pedal hub, not behind it.

- **In-line skating and cross-country skiing.** Chart a course that keeps you working steadily, with no long coasting or steep inclines. Otherwise, the aerobic training effect is interrupted.

- **Water running.** This activity uses a cross-country ski action in water neck deep or deeper. Water running is probably the best aerobic activity for players who are having hip, knee, or ankle problems that restrict their land-training efforts. The water is gentle on the joints while providing sufficient resistance to meet aerobic criterion. Be sure to move through a full range of motion in the running stride and arm action. Use the water resistance in both directions. As on land, play with pace to get a good sense of easy, moderate, and strong.

Chapter 8

Speed

"Maybe you'll work hard and not make it. But if you don't work hard, you know you won't make it."—
John R. Johnson's mother

Speed is the toughest aspect of fitness to train because the training hurts. You have to push until your muscles are loaded with lactic acid. Speed training produces a hockey player who can go hard every shift of every period. A player with speed becomes extremely valuable toward the end of each period, especially the third, and for overtime.

The speed-training drills used in *52-Week Hockey Training* require one thing to be effective. You must go all out for the work phases every time. (See figure 7.1, rate of perceived exertion scale, in chapter 7.) All out in your training is 18 to 19 (extremely hard) on the scale. If you pace yourself because you have six reps to do, you will not improve. Going all out means that you must take advantage of the rest phases. Go very easy in the rest phases but do not sit or stand still. Gentle movement will flush the lactic acid from your muscles more effectively than no activity at all.

All speed drills specify the work-to-rest intervals and the number of times you should repeat the work-to-rest cycle. For example, a drill may be indicated as "(30:60) 4 reps." The units are seconds, with the first number indicating the work portion and the second the rest portion. This example means that you go all out for 30 seconds and rest for 60 seconds, repeating the combination until you have competed four reps nonstop (e.g., 30:60:30:60:30:60:30:60).

An important note about the work-rest regimes is that it is far more critical that you maintain an all-out work effort as you complete repeats than that you stay with the prescribed work-rest ratio. In other words, if you're asked to do six reps of 30:60 and you can't keep the fourth rep at the pace of the first three, then lengthen the rest ratio so that you can do the fifth rep near the original pace. If you can't, doing the sixth rep at a slower pace is a waste of time.

These principles are the same whether you are speed training off-ice or on-ice. Observing these principles is especially important when doing on-ice drills to get maximum transfer of training to game skills. When the purpose of a drill is speed training in combination with a skill like passing, push the speed and let the skill catch up, not the other way around. If you don't push the speed, you nullify the training effect.

Track running, treadmill running, and stationary cycling are the most practical activities for off-ice speed training. For on-ice drills, good starts and stops and skating technique are essential to being able to hold the work pace. In addition, be sure to warm up sufficiently before you start any speed drills.

Speed training produces a player who can play hard throughout the game, thus proving very valuable to the team.

Off-Ice Speed Drills

Ladder Drill

Start with a loose jog or easy pedal speed. Then go all out (work) for 10 seconds, rest for 20 seconds, work for 20 seconds, rest for 30 seconds, work for 20 seconds, rest for 20 seconds, work for 20 seconds, rest for 10 seconds, work for 10 seconds, rest for 70 seconds. Start with 4 repeats. As you improve, increase gradually to 8 reps.

Short Shift

Do 30 seconds of work followed by 30 seconds of rest. Start with 6 reps and gradually increase to 10.

Long Shift

Do 45 seconds of work followed by 45 seconds of rest. Start with 4 reps and gradually increase to 8.

On-Ice Speed Drills

Line Ladder Drill

Refer to the illustration. Solid lines represent the work effort. Dotted lines are rests, but you blast across the last blue line first. When a turn is required, perform it using a stop and start, always facing the penalty box. Start at pylon 1 and after each rest interval, move up a pylon. After doing 4 work back down to 1. That sequence completes one repetition. Rest (skate easy laps) for one minute and then repeat four to eight cycles. Players can go one at a time, starting as soon as the player ahead crosses the first blue line. Be sure to shift to the next lane on each turn so that you don't run into an incoming player.

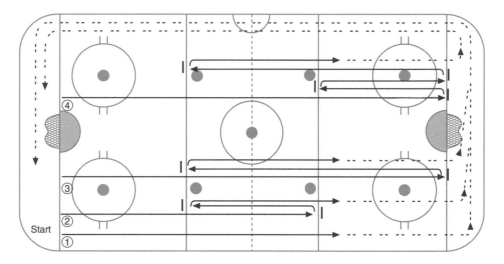

Short Shift

Use the width of the ice and stops and starts at the boards, facing the same end of the ice each turn, for the 30-second work intervals. Skate easy laps for the 30-second rest intervals. Do 6 to 10 repeats.

Long Shift

Use the same skating pattern as you did for the short-shift drill, but intervals are 45 seconds of work and 45 seconds of rest. Do four to eight repeats.

On-Ice Positional Speed Drills

Forward Attack Drill

F1, F2, and F3 start at center. F1 passes to either F2 or F3 as all three attack the goal. They continue with the same puck until they score or the goalie freezes the puck. Then all quickly return to the neutral zone to get a second puck and repeat the drill. Continue until the line has used four pucks or attacked for at least 30 seconds. The next line begins immediately. Rotate lines for four to six repeats.

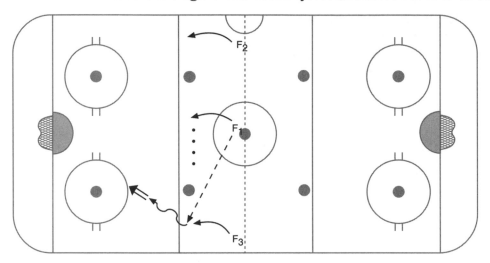

Forward Challenge Drill

This is a 1-on-0, 2-on-0, 3-on-0, 3-on-1, 3-on-2 drill. F1 attacks one goalie for a shot while F2 and F3 go 2-on-0 against the far goalie. After a shot, F1 picks up a puck below the goal line as F2 and F3 join F1. F1, F2, and F3 attack the far goal 3-on-0. D1 follows F1, F2, and F3 into the zone and picks up F1, F2, and F3 for a 3-on-1 in the opposite direction. D2 and D3 follow the play to start a 3-on-2 back. The next forward line starts as soon as the 3-on-2 is dead. Rotate lines for four to six repeats.

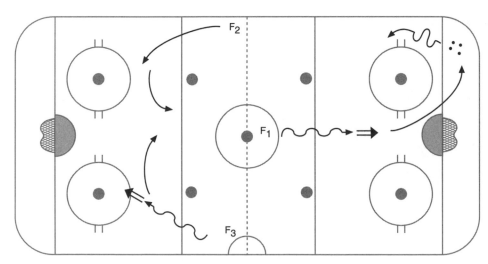

Defense Net Drill

D1 starts in front of the net, uses a quick pivot, and drives hard to the left corner, touching the boards with the stick and stopping. The player back skates to the start position, pivots to the opposite corner, and returns to the start. D1 quickly skates to the top of the left face-off circle, stops, back skates to the start, and stops. The player quickly skates to the top of the right circle and returns. D1 repeats the sequence for 30 seconds, and then the next defenseman starts immediately. Rotate through defensemen for four to six repeats.

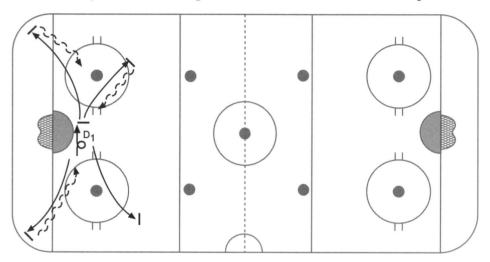

Defense Get-Out Drill

D1 and D2 start at the blue line. The coach dumps a puck into the corner. D1 goes to the net as D2 retrieves the puck. D1 and D2 skate aggressively out of the zone with the puck and pass it to the coach. The coach dumps the puck into the opposite corner as D1 and D2 repeat the drill. They work for 30 seconds. The next defensive pair then starts immediately. Rotate through pairs for four to six repeats.

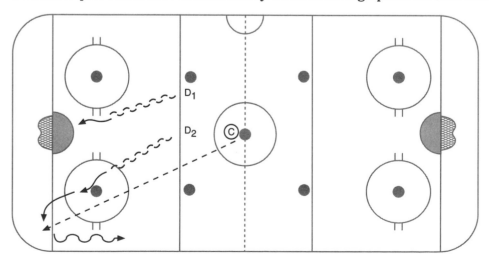

Forwards and Defense 3-on-2 Switch Drill

F1, F2, and F3 attack D3 and D4, 3-on-2 in one zone. At the same time F4, F5, and F6 attack D1 and D2, 3-on-2 in the other zone. Coaches add pucks in each zone to continue the 3-on-2 battles. After 10 seconds a coach blows a whistle. Each forward line then attacks the opposite end. On the whistle the defensive pairs must gain the blue line at their end to defend against the new line. Repeat for three switches, then rest 60 to 90 seconds.

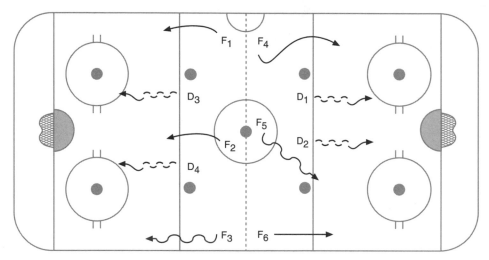

Goaltenders' Five-Point Shooting

X1, X2, X3, X4, and X5 each have two pucks. X1 shoots a puck, X2 shoots a puck, and so on until X5 shoots. Then X1 starts a repeat (for a total of 10 shots). Players should allow the goalie to face the puck before shooting a quick-release shot. The goalie then rests for 60 seconds (rotate goalies). Repeat four to six times.

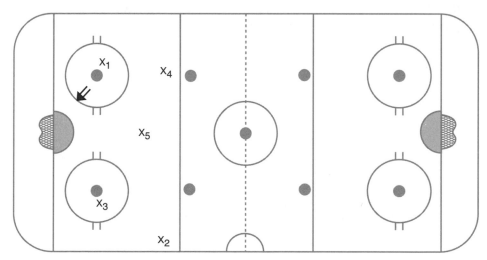

Combination Speed-Skill Drills

3-on-2 in-the-Zone Drill

F1, F2, and F3 start at center. D1 and D2 start outside the blue line. F1, F2, and F3 pick up a puck from the center-ice circle and attack D1 and D2, 3-on-2. F1, F2, and F3 continue the attack until they score or D1 and D2 clear the puck out of the zone. F1, F2, and F3 then retrieve the next puck from the center-ice circle and repeat. All attacks must be onside and maintain high intensity for at least 30 seconds. The next forward and defense unit then go for 30 seconds. Use both ends of the ice.

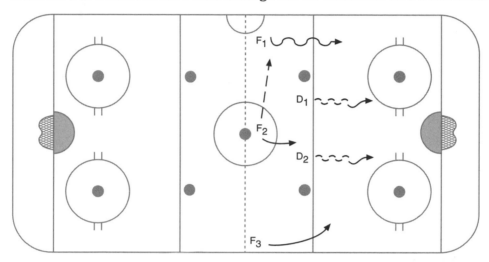

3-on-3 Cross-Zone Drill

Move the goal nets to play cross ice in one end. Divide players into two teams. A coach dumps the puck into the zone for 3-on-3 cross ice. Use both ends if you have extra players. Go to 2-on-2 if intensity is insufficient. Do 45-second shifts of all-out effort.

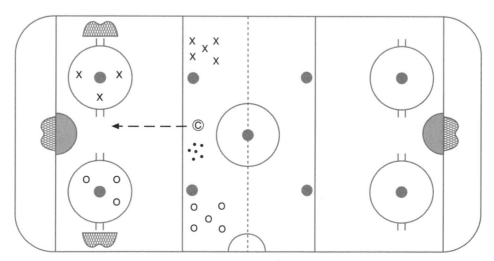

Continuous Scrimmage

Use full-ice 5-on-5 for 30-second shifts with no play stoppages. On a whistle the team with the puck passes it to their goalie and changes with new lines coming off the bench. Continue until each unit has had four to eight shifts. Go for maximum intensity and good puck and player movement. The drill can be done 4-on-4. You can set the maximum time a player can control the puck (e.g., three seconds) before having to pass or shoot.

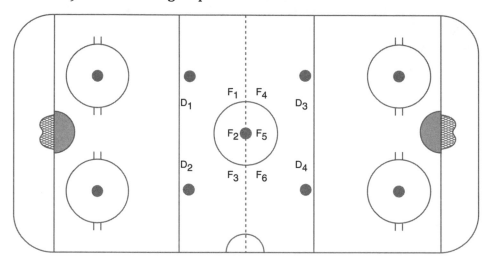

Alternative Speed-Training Drills

Line Running (Off-Ice)

The lines of a football field or basketball court offer a convenient setting for speed training with starts and stops. Vary the target line for each out and back and make the total run last 30 to 60 seconds. The rest interval should be equal to or as much as double the work interval. Use four to eight repeats.

Pylon Skate (On-Ice)

Place pylons on the ice as indicated in the illustration. Players start to skate all out from behind the net, going around the outside of each pylon until they return to the starting end. They skate full speed throughout. Repeats start on 90-second intervals so that the faster players skate, the more rest they get. The next player starts when the previous player reaches the second pylon. Repeat 4 to 10 times.

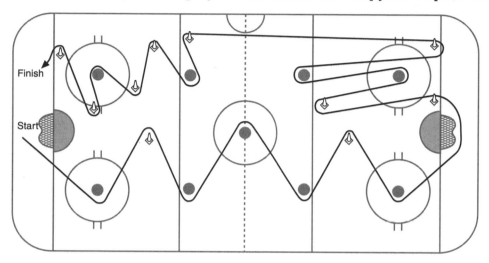

Chapter 9

Power and Quickness

"Perseverance is not a long race; it is many short races one after another."—***Walter Elliott***

Power and quickness are the easiest aspects of fitness to train. Ten minutes each day and voila! There is no excuse for a player to be slow afoot or to have a slow shot release. Like speed training, however, the training for power and quickness must be done right to be effective.

Power and quickness training must be explosive. (See figure 7.1, rate of perceived exertion scale, in chapter 7.) Explosive means a pace of 20 (maximal exertion) on the RPE scale. Nothing less during a work interval will give you improvement. For that reason, if in successive repeats you find that you are performing at a pace that is less than explosive, you should either lengthen the rest intervals or reduce the number of repeats.

The work-to-rest ratios are specified with two numbers, for example, "10:50," which means to explode for 10 seconds and then go very easy for 50 seconds. Occasionally, a drill is prescribed as "on 1 min," which means to explode throughout one cycle of the drill and then take the balance of that minute to rest. Start the next repeat at the start of the next minute. The quicker you do the drill, the more rest you get.

As with speed training, these principles apply whether you work on-ice or off-ice. The on-ice work is critical for getting power and quickness to transfer to specific hockey skills. But you must adhere to one order of concentration to optimize the transfer. Concentrate first on your pace in doing the drills. Focus second on the perfection. For example, in the puck bash drill, your primary focus must be on the pace of your release on the shots, not on accuracy. If you focus on accuracy first, you compromise the explosive requirement of power and quickness training. Once you ingrain the pace of release, go for greater accuracy, but make sure you hold the explosive pace. This order will ultimately provide you with powerful, quick-release, accurate shots.

Off-Ice Power and Quickness Drills

Power Push-Ups

Start by lying on your stomach with your hands under your shoulders and your toes on the floor. Push up fast and hard, keeping your body straight so that your hands leave the floor after your elbows and wrists extend (level I). Tap your chest after your hands leave the floor (level II). Catch and control your descent in each push-up.

Tuck Jumps

From a standing position with your feet shoulder-width apart, jump vertically as high as possible. At the top of the jump, draw your knees to your chest and then extend to cushion your landing (level I). A subsequent jump follows the first immediately (no bounce). For level II, do the same tuck jump from a position standing on only one leg. After a complete set, repeat for the other leg.

Lateral Line Jumps

Place four lines of tape on the floor as indicated in the illustration, each one foot (30 centimeters) apart. Start in the center on both feet (level I) and jump the pattern as quickly as possible. A count of "right-two-three-two-left-two-three-two," in which the numbers are the number of lines you jump over, may help your rhythm and direction, which alternates unless called otherwise. Level II is the same pattern using jumps from only one leg. Switch legs after each set.

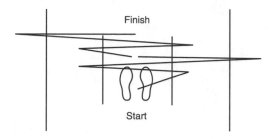

Incline Blast

Use a long run of stairs going three at a stride or use a moderately sloped hill and long strides. Explode up the incline for the work interval and walk back down for the rest interval. Repeat 6 to 12 times.

Arm Step-Ups

Start in the up phase of a push-up position, facing a step or an 8- to 10-inch (20- to 25-centimeter) box. Use your arms to step on and off the box in a cycle of right up, left up, right down, left down. Go as fast as possible. Alternate the starting arm in subsequent repeats. Do 6 to 12 repeats.

On-Ice Power and Quickness Drills

Puck Bash

Blast 10 to 12 pucks in rapid succession at a target. Use a forehand snap shot for the first rep, then alternate with a backhand set for the required number of reps. Remember that pace is more important than accuracy at first. Do 6 to 12 reps. Distance from the target will vary.

Slot Drill

The player starts 10 feet (3 meters) out from a target with another player shadow checking the first. Two partners stand on either side of the target (e.g., blue line on boards) and alternately feed pucks to the player, who tries to get free of the checker to shoot each feed on target. The player uses short, quick, high-intensity maneuvering for 10 seconds, then rests. Rest means that players rotate positions. Repeat for 6 to 12 rotations.

Circle Shuttle

Start in the center dot of a circle. Move explosively in every direction throughout the pattern shown in the illustration, going in order through directions 1 through 4. Rest while three or four teammates do the drill, then do your next rep. Go approximately once per minute. Do 6 to 12 repeats.

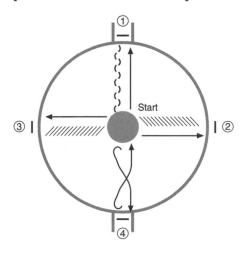

Center Shuttle

Explode through each leg of the pattern shown in the illustration, using stops, turns, and starts as indicated. Turn so that you always face the penalty box. Rest after crossing the last blue line for the duration of the allotted time. Repeat 6 to 12 times.

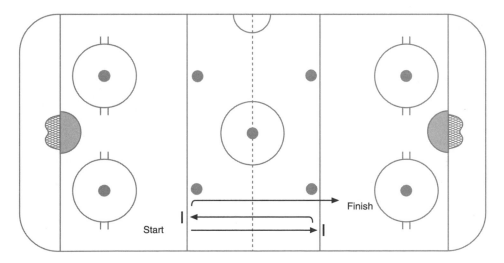

On-Ice Positional Power and Quickness Drills

Forward Shooting Drill

F1 drives down the wall for a shot off the wing. F2 comes out of the corner for a wraparound. F3 comes across the slot for a quick-release shot. The second rotation starts from the opposite side and opposite corner. Work for 10 seconds and rest for 50 seconds, or rest as the second and third lines work.

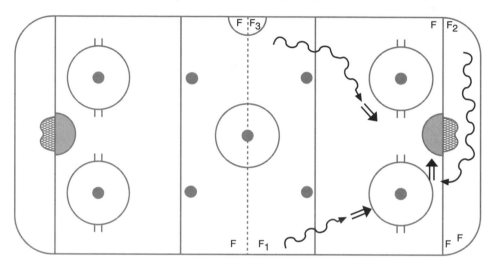

Forward Quick-Corner Drill

F1 drives down the wall for a shot off the wing. After the shot F1 must retrieve a puck from the corner for a second shot on goal. F1 then retrieves the puck from the other corner for a third shot. After the third shot F1 skates hard to gain the blue line. F2 goes when F1 is out of the zone. Repeat 6 to 10 times. Use both ends of the ice.

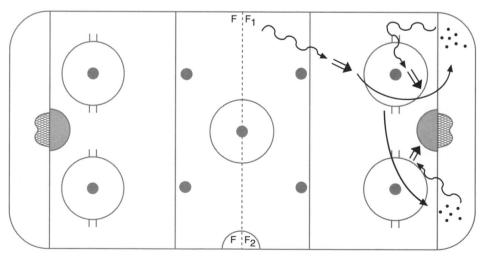

Defense Walk-and-Shoot Drill

D goes down the boards, picks up a puck, and skates backward to the blue line. D uses crossovers to gain a shooting angle for a shot on goal (walk and shoot). Repeat 6 to 10 times, alternating with a partner.

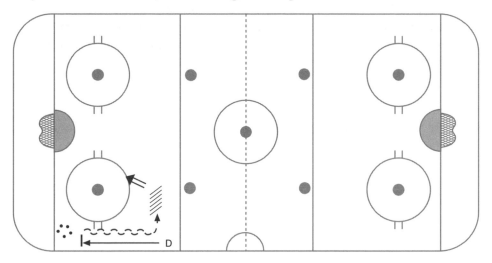

Defense 1-on-1 Quick-Up Drill

On a whistle, D1, D2, F1, and F2 leave. D1 must skate backward to the blue line, pivot, and pick up a puck. D1 passes to F2. Then D1 must skate above the pylon, pivot, and play F1 1-on-1. (The diagram shows only D1 and F2.) Go on the whistle. Repeat 6 to 10 times, rotating with teammates.

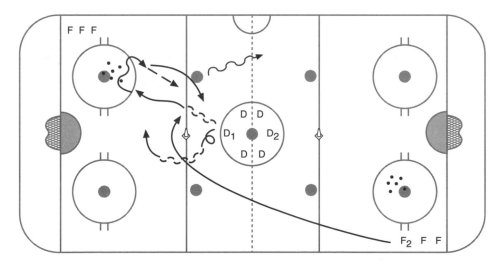

Forward and Defense Your Shot Drill

F skates in a figure-8 around pylons, starting from the boards side of the pylons and finishing with a drive to the net for a shot on goal. D starts with a puck on the outside of the pylons, pivots on the top of the pylons, back skates back through the pylons to the blue line, and pivots for crossovers along the blue line for a shot on goal. Explode through the drill. Repeat 6 to 10 times. Forward and defenseman line up on the same side of the ice and alternate shots. The line then moves to shoot from the other side of the ice.

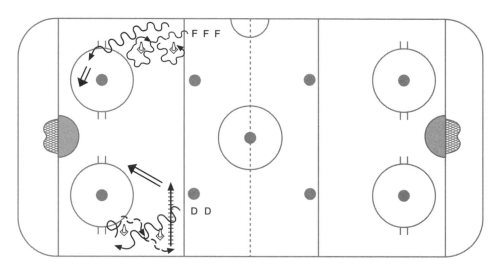

Goaltenders' Scramble Drill

Start in the center of the goal crease. Do all actions as though making saves in a barrage. Drop to knees or butterfly. Return to the start position. Kick save to the left. Move back to the start position. Dive save to the right. Move back to the start position. Drop to back save. Move up to the start position. Repeat this cycle for the prescribed duration, then rest. Do 6 to 12 repeats.

Goaltenders' Telescoping

The goalie starts in the crease. A coach stands in line with the center-ice dot and numbers the two end face-off dots and neutral-zone dots. The coach calls out a dot number. The goalie challenges that dot as if a shooter were shooting from that spot. The goalie quickly returns to the crease start position, ready to react to a shot from the next dot number.

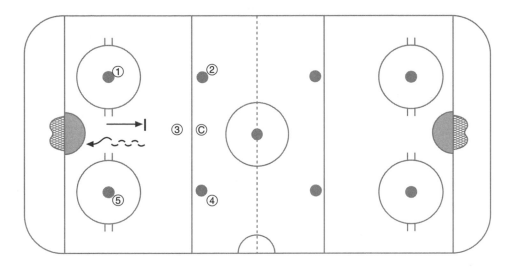

Goaltenders' Down-Up Shot Drill

X1 lines up six pucks for rapid fire. The goalie starts in proper stance and drops to his knees. As the goalie is returning to standing stance, X1 shoots. The goalie repeats the down-up action on each shot as X1 continues rapid fire until all pucks have been shot. Rest 50 seconds. Repeat 6 to 10 times.

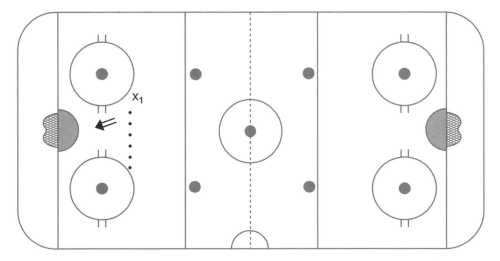

Goaltenders' Lateral-Movement Drill

Place three pucks along the goal line on each side of the net. The goalie starts at the post on X1's side of the net. X1 passes to X3 for a quick-release shot. Immediately after playing the shot, the goalie goes to X2's post. Repeat for six shots. Rest 30 to 60 seconds. Repeat 6 to 10 times.

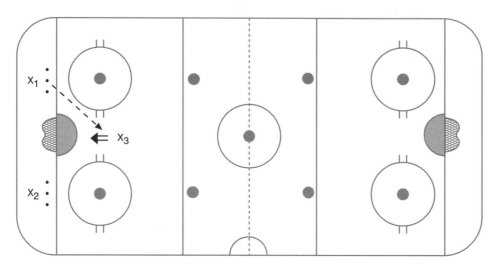

Goaltenders' Wraparound Drill

X1 leaves from below the goal line and goes behind the net for a wraparound shot on goal. X2 leaves from the opposite corner when X1 shoots. The goalie must make a quick lateral move across the crease to make saves. The goalie works for six shots or 10 seconds. The second goaltender then moves into the crease. Repeat 6 to 10 times.

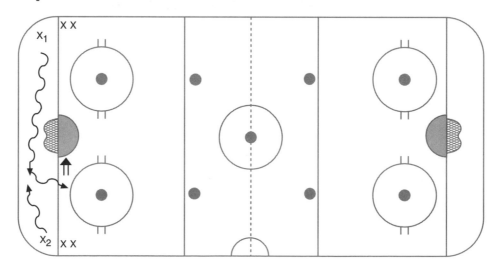

Combination Power-Quickness-Skill Drills

Figure-8 Pass Drill

X1 faces X2 through the entire drill. X1 skates a figure-8 around the pylons. X2 passes the puck to X1 every time X1 pivots around a pylon and is between the pylons. X1 immediately returns the puck to X2. Work 10 seconds and rest 50 seconds. Repeat 6 to 10 times.

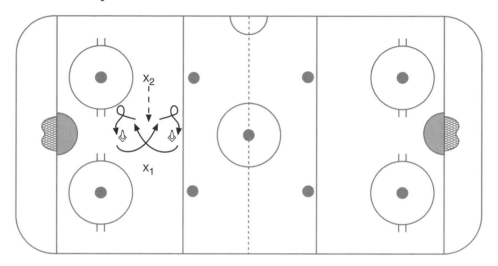

Quick-Shot Drill

X1 leaves from the corner with a puck and skates above the top of the circle for a quick-release shot. After the shot X1 picks up a second puck below the goal line and skates above the opposite circle for a second shot. X2 passes to X1 for a third shot immediately after the second shot. X2 then follows the same sequence. Repeat 6 to 10 times, rotating with four to six teammates.

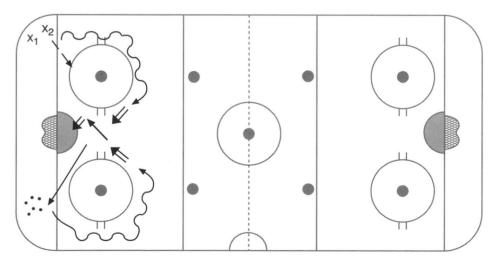

Quick-Release Drill

X1 skates through pylons following a figure-8 pattern, always facing the net. As X1 comes between the pylons and faces X3 or X2, one of them passes to X1 for a quick release, alternating passes as X1 pivots around the pylons. After 10 seconds X2 changes with X1 to become the shooter. After 10 seconds X2 changes with X3. Repeat 6 to 10 times.

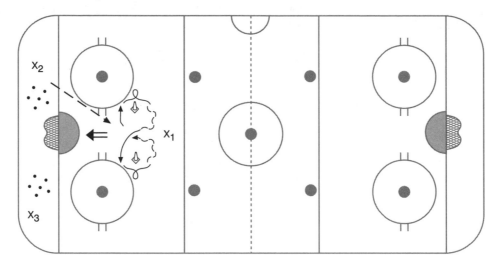

Alternative Power and Quickness Drills

Double Step-Ups (Off-Ice)

Use the bottom two steps of a staircase or a step box of two stairs. As quickly as possible, step your right foot on step one, left foot on step two, right foot on step two, left foot on step one, right foot to start, left foot to start. Work for 10 seconds and rest for 50 seconds. Lead with your left leg for the next repeat. Do 6 to 12 reps.

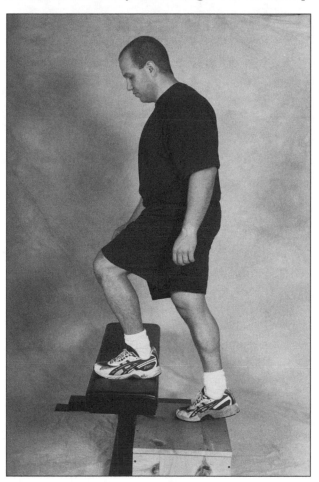

On-the-Spot Quick Feet (Off-Ice)

As quickly as possible, run on the spot four steps, hop to straddle position, hop to right-front crossover, hop to straddle, hop to left-front crossover, run on the spot four steps, hop to right-forward-left-back straddle, hop feet together, hop to left-forward-right-back straddle, hop feet together. That sequence completes one cycle. Repeat the cycle for 10 seconds, then rest for 50 seconds. Do 6 to 12 repeats.

Box Skate (On-Ice)

Skate the following sequence explosively in the box pattern outlined in the illustration, starting with the outer sequence. Skate forward, cross over (in front/behind) left, skate backward, cross over right, give one maximal push off the right leg for one stride to the diagonal corner, turn right to skate forward, cross over right, skate backward, cross over left, and give one maximal push off the left leg for one stride to the diagonal corner (starting corner). Start this sequence on one-minute intervals. Repeat 6 to 12 times.

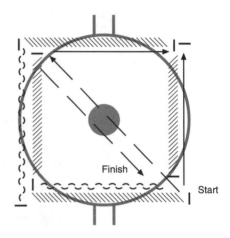

Puck Snap (On-Ice)

Place six pucks on both your forehand and backhand sides about seven feet (two meters) from a target (e.g., the blue line on boards). Alternately snap one forehand shot and then one backhand shot as quickly as possible until all pucks are gone (worry about accuracy later). Rest for 30 to 60 seconds. Repeat 6 to 12 times.

About the Authors

Don MacAdam is head coach and director of hockey operations for the Charlotte Checkers. A former professional ice hockey player himself, MacAdam has more than 25 years of coaching experience at various elite levels, including teams in the National Hockey League (Detroit Red Wings), the American Hockey League (Edmonton Oilers and Ottawa Senators Farm Teams), the IHL (Milwaukee Admirals), Major Junior (500 Greyhounds), and the Japan Ice Hockey League (the Nippon Paper Cranes), as well as several minor-league teams. He has also served as a consultant with Canada's world championship team, evaluating NHL players as candidates for Team Canada and coaching the team during the Bauer Cup.

MacAdam is the coauthor of three previous hockey conditioning books: *The Hockey Conditioning Handbook, How to Make the Best Use of Your Ice Time,* and *Hockey Fitness: Year-Round Conditioning On and Off the Ice.* With a special focus on conditioning for the sport, he lectures at hockey clinics throughout Canada and the United States.

MacAdam earned his master's degree in physical education from the University of New Brunswick. He currently lives in Charlotte, North Carolina. His interests include home renovation, carpentry, reading, biking, hiking, and playing golf.

Gail Reynolds is an exercise physiologist who has been developing training programs for amateur and elite hockey players and teams over the past 22 years, including NHL stars. A former professor of exercise physiology at the University of New Brunswick, she currently runs her own fitness consulting company.

A member of the committee that developed Canada's coaching certification program, Reynolds has also spoken at several Canadian Amateur Hockey Association Level 4 and 5 clinics and lectured at the York symposium for elite coaches. Her articles have appeared in *Coaching Review* and the *Journal of Applied Physiology.*

Reynolds earned her master's degree in physical education from the University of Western Ontario, where she specialized in exercise physiology and psychology. She lives in Ingersoll, Ontario, where she enjoys hiking with her dogs, writing sports fiction, and renovating and landscaping her home.

Maximize Your Workouts

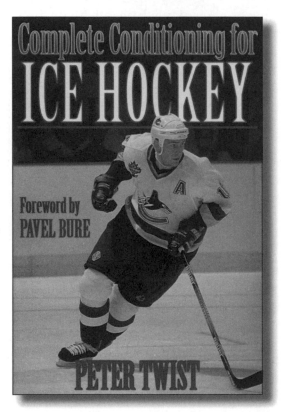

256 pages • ISBN 0-87322-887-1

Improve your strength, speed, agility, and endurance with *Complete Conditioning for Ice Hockey*. Peter Twist, NHL strength and conditioning coach, provides 125 of the best on- and off-ice training exercises and drills for getting into rock-hard hockey shape.

Plus, sample practice sessions and conditioning programs will help players of all ages and skill levels maximize their training. This fully illustrated guide includes:

- 23 stretches for flexibility,
- 8 on-ice activities for aerobic and anaerobic training,
- 37 on- and off-ice strengthening exercises,
- 35 drills and activities to develop quickness and agility, and
- 22 speed-training drills to add power to skating.

Numerous NHL stars, including Trevor Linden, Mike Peca, Jyrki Lumme, and Geoff Courtnall demonstrate the exercises in detailed photos. All-stars Wayne Gretzky, Steve Larmer, Doug Gilmour, and others discuss what hockey conditioning has meant to their success, and offer tips to aspiring players.

Get *Complete Conditioning for Ice Hockey* and get in top shape for today's fast, physical game.

HUMAN KINETICS

The Premier Publisher for Sports & Fitness

P.O. Box 5076, Champaign, IL 61825-5076

2335